To Helen
with love,
marg
Summer, 1984

The Passionate Observer

Donald Creighton
The Passionate Observer

Selected Writings

McCLELLAND AND STEWART

The Canadian Publishers
McClelland and Stewart Limited
25 Hollinger Road
Toronto   M4B 3G2

Canadian Cataloguing in Publication Data

Creighton, Donald, 1902-1979.
   The passionate observer

ISBN 0-7710-2363-4

1. Canada – Social life and customs – 20th century – Addresses, essays, lectures.*
2. Canada – Social conditions – Addresses, essays, lectures.   I. Title.

FC89.C73   971   C80-094570-0
F1021.2.C73

Printed and bound in the United States of America

Contents

PART THREE

Introduction

When I first met Donald Creighton in 1969, it was as editor of *Canada's First Century*, which he had just finished for Macmillan. I knew him to be the outstanding narrative historian of the country, but soon recognized that his genius and temperament were predominantly artistic, a realization that put into gratifying perspective his powerful, highly sensitive, and strongly reactive personality. Scholarship and dedicated teaching were the foundation of his reputation as an historian, but it was his talent as a writer which preoccupied him and which lifted him to his unique level of accomplishment.

We became friends, and over the next ten years I saw him frequently, often to go to the theatre or the opera, which he particularly loved. He was a stimulating companion on these occasions, enthusiastic and responsive, capable of being driven out of a theatre by something he disliked, and of being moved to tears by scenes which appealed to him. Once, at a performance of *Der Rosenkavalier* – it was the last opera Donald saw – he was quite overcome towards the end of the first act. Here, in a passage of great beauty and profundity, which emerges from a plot of frothy frivolity, the heroine, acknowledging the passage of time, and her own aging, sings:

Time is a strange thing.
When one lives heedlessly time means nothing.
But then suddenly one is aware of nothing else.
It is all around us, it is also inside us.

*Time, too, is a creation of the Father who
has created us all.**

Donald was deeply moved by this scene, not only, I think, because
of its acknowledgement of mortality, but also because of his own
concern for the force of time, which he saw as an artist and an
historian. In his essay "History and Literature" he wrote:

> Time is the essence of history; and any young student who
> wants to be an historian and hasn't a sensitive feeling for
> time – for growth and change and decay – had better alter his
> plans and take up a timeless and lifeless study such as
> political science or economic theory.†

Certainly a sensitive feeling for time is one of the features of his
writing and often it became the major dynamic force in a book or
essay.

Editing Donald Creighton's work was an easy task since he was
such an extraordinarily good writer. The soundness and assurance
of his prose, and the overall structure of his ideas, were
exceptional, and it was rare to find anything that was superfluous
or incomplete, or that could be expressed with more clarity or
arranged to better advantage.

Donald was not a trained musician but his strong musicality
contributed to his writing style; he was as sensitive to the balance
and rhythm of his sentences as he was to the accuracy and power
of his choice of words and the liveliness and suitability of his
imagery, and he was most responsive to editorial suggestions
relating to style. He hated other people fiddling with his prose, and
with good reason; the results were rarely an improvement. On the
other hand, he was often more than willing to tailor his writing to
meet a particular commission or request.

The literary skills which he brought to historical writing were

---

* Translation by Walter Legge, © 1957 International Music Establishment

† *Towards the Discovery of Canada*, Toronto, 1972, page 23.

broadly based. He was familiar with a great body of French and English literature, and from childhood knew by heart many of the great English poems. In his writing, the spectacular set pieces, characterizations, and atmospherics that feature in his major works are thought of as his literary aspects. But equally effective is his wonderful capacity for synthesizing information; quantities of statistics, logistics, and subsidiary issues are deftly subsumed into the narrative and made part of the whole.

He was a Mozartian kind of artist, in the sense that his writing, once begun, proceeded with great assurance. When the real work had been done – the research completed, the imagination engaged, and the book or essay conceived – the actual writing was very quick; his hand would swiftly cover page after page with his steady, consistent script. Certainly there were occasional changes, and the odd false start, but for the most part, his original drafts are remarkably clean and regular in appearance. *Dominion of the North* was written in a year and a half; both volumes of *John A. Macdonald* "wrote themselves quickly," as he put it, though they were, of course, preceded by years of research. This speed and confidence stayed with him until his last year, when purely physical limitations began to slow his writing down.

Donald Creighton loved writing. It was a childhood passion and it remained his major interest and activity until the end of his life. He also enjoyed the publishing process and was proud that all twelve of his books, with publication dates spanning forty years, were still in print. Book publishers played an important part in his career, influencing the choice of subject and approach of some of his work, and several became close friends, including John Gray, the long-time president of the Macmillan Company of Canada, Lovat Dickson, the writer and former managing director of the British Macmillan Company, and Jack McClelland. Donald was constantly interested in the activities of the literary and publishing worlds, and he was a member of the Writers' Union of Canada.

Literature was an interest he shared with his wife Luella, and it was during the course of their long marriage that they both became authors, she a novelist and writer of popular history. When they moved from Toronto to a Victorian house in Brooklin, Ontario, they added a wing which gave each of them a writing room, one above the other.

In this collection there are a number of pieces which are not included for the frustrating reason that they were never written. Donald did not have strong autobiographical instincts as he thought his life would not be of general interest – this was not an expression of modesty or regret, merely the judgement of a writer and critic. He occasionally sketched out the course of his professional career, as in his piece on Eugene Forsey, reprinted in this collection, or in the introduction to *Towards the Discovery of Canada*.

He should have been encouraged to write down some of the vignettes that often arose in his conversation, about his family background and his experiences, such as recollections of his powerful, forward-looking grandmother, or his time in Rhodesia with the Monckton Commission, or his encounter with Lord Beaverbrook, who used his considerable histrionic skills in an attempt (unsuccessful) to persuade Donald to undertake a biography of R.B. Bennett. Then there were his early visits to France. As did a number of other distinguished writers, Donald had spent "that summer" – 1928 – in Paris. Accompanied by his recent bride Luella, and intent on historical research, he did not, like John Glassco, pursue outré amours, or, like Morley Callaghan, box with Hemingway, but he could give comparable vivid descriptions of aspects of his life there, such as a wonderful evocation of the atmosphere at the Bibliothèque Nationale, where he was doing his research, which, on hot days, became fetid and required the services of a man with a deodorant spray gun. Better still was his recollection of the performances of the great Paris music hall artists. He could sing verse after verse of their songs, and to have Mistinguette or Chevalier recreated out of Donald's rather gothic demeanour at luncheon in Brooklin, was a startling pleasure.

This collection of writing was being put together by Donald Creighton before he died, in December 1979. Although he did not make the final selection and arrangement, the idea and the general range of contents are his. The pieces included here were, with one exception, written after 1971, when, having spent over forty years on the staff of the University of Toronto, he finally retired from university life. He now worked and wrote almost entirely in Brooklin, or at the Creightons' summer cottage in Muskoka. As he got older, active archival historical research became impossible, but in this period he completed three books: *Canada: the Heroic Beginnings, The Forked Road*, and his only work of fiction, *Takeover*. Writing *Takeover* was a great pleasure to him, for he had had a lifetime ambition to write novels, and a particular fascination with the classic thriller genre. At the time he died, he had a new novel under way, as well as a major essay, which was intended for this book.

As can be seen from the range of subject matter of the pieces here, after 1971 he was enjoying a career as a more general writer and man of letters. The selections have been arranged in three parts: the first contains articles of a contemporary political nature; the second reflects his literary interests; and the third includes his essays on personalities in the academic world.

Donald Creighton became well-known as a writer and speaker on current political issues comparatively late in his career; there is a sense in which he had written Canadian history from beginning to end before coming to grips with the present. *Canada's First Century*, which was published in 1970, concluded with a pessimistic and challenging prognosis for Canada's likely national survival. These nationalist views, which he had held for a good many years, now found a new and much wider popular following, and somewhat fortuitously, he became recognized as one of the leaders of the nationalist movement of the early 1970s. He also became convinced of the related importance of conservationist and environmental concerns. The first three articles deal with these matters, of which the third, "Preserving the Peaceable Kingdom," published now for the first time, is one of Donald's most graceful and positive statements about the value of our political institutions.

The essay here titled "Beyond the Referendum" deals with Quebec. When this piece originally appeared in *Maclean's* magazine, it produced a huge reader response, lost him a few friends, and gained him many new admirers. His frustration over the question of Quebec and Canada was not new. Forty years earlier, in his first book, *The Empire of the St. Lawrence*, he wrote of how the power of the old trading empire of British North America had been defeated in part by centrifugal Quebec forces.

Two short articles on very different issues conclude this section. The spectacular polemic, "The Politics of Pickering," was written at the time of the People or Planes movement against the Pickering airport. Since the proposed airport was to be located very close to the village of Brooklin, the subject had a certain personal concern. "Wine, Spirits, and Provincial Politicians" is a hilarious brief history of the Liquor Control Board of Ontario. Why did he write it? I never got around to asking him, but I imagine that it came out of the research he did for his novel, in which the takeover in question is of a fine old Ontario family distillery.

The group of pieces on literary subjects begins with a spirited attack on book reviewing conventions in Canada, and particularly in the *Globe and Mail*, where the article originally appeared. Delighted to be sprung from the confines of historical reviewing, Donald wrote a number of literary reviews for that paper, mainly on writers of the past whom he particularly admired. As a reviewer, both historical and otherwise, he was principled and positive-minded. He had a fundamental respect for good writers, and though his praise was never fulsome, he was generous and enthusiastic, and he was capable (as in the Monsarrat review) of appreciating the virtues of a book he did not himself enjoy.

Donald Creighton's early experience of literature and the world of publishing can be seen in his account of his father's career as editor of the United Church's newspapers. It was written for the present-day United Church *Observer*, though in fact never published. In Donald's view, his father's quarrel with senior members of the United Church over the issue of Moral Rearmament was decisive and rather tragic. Since the Church does not come out of the story well, the essay has a somewhat combative tone that doesn't get us very close to the relations between father and son.

In the section on academic subjects, the essay "Macdonald,

Baldwin, and the University of Toronto," which has not been published before, is the special lecture he gave at the University of Toronto, during its sesquicentennial year. He had been asked to speak on the historical setting of the founding of the university, and he did so, giving a characteristic example of his virtuoso historical writing: out of a welter of confused stories and information comes a good story, a cogent synthesis of the facts and a lively depiction of the personalities and their relationships.

"The Ogdensburg Agreement and F.H. Underhill," a more recent episode in university history, originally appeared, somewhat anomalously, in the collection of essays called *The West and the Nation*, published in honour of Donald's friend and fellow historian, W.L. Morton. The rivalry between Underhill and Creighton is an oft-told story in university circles, but here the tone seems more jocose than aggressive.

The accounts of Donald's colleagues and friends, Innis, Brebner, Stacey, and Forsey, are brief biographies written with a fine eye for narrative line. The paper on Harold Innis, Donald Creighton's friend and mentor, has not been published before. It presents some views and opinions additional to those expressed in his affectionate biography of Innis, published in 1957. The essays on Innis, Stacey, and Forsey, in particular, reveal the enormous pleasure Donald Creighton got out of his friendships. He had a deep interest and curiosity in his friends, in their characters and their roles in life. Selective, emotionally responsive, and highly charged, his friendships remained lively and dynamic, as did his delight in good company and good conversation, preferably accompanied by good food and wine.

The pieces in this collection were originally written for different occasions and appeared in a variety of publications, but they all have a constancy of vision and style that is the mark of Donald Creighton's work. This vision was sometimes pessimistic, but the energy and passion and assurance he brought to his writing, gave new vitality to every subject and issue he turned to.

Ramsay Derry
July 1980

The
Passionate
Observer

Part One

The Future in Canada

In a witty talk, which he gave on the future of Christmas, the novelist Robertson Davies suggested that prophets ought to be given the greatest latitude. I am going to ask a similar indulgence, but not in virtue of my prophetic powers. I am not a prophet or the son of a prophet. I am supposed, by profession, to be an historian, and the business of history, almost everybody, including most historians, agrees is the past, not the future. Many people would even argue that history, by its very name and nature, is utterly incapable of giving us the slightest indication of what lies ahead. "The light which experience gives," Samuel Taylor Coleridge once wrote, "is a lantern on the stern, which shines only on the water behind us." Literally, of course, this is quite true; but the waves behind the vessel which is carrying humanity forward into the unknown, are not entirely without meaning for the future. They can teach us where the winds of change are blowing and on what course the chief currents of our age are set. They can reveal to us the main direction of our voyage through time. Of course, the trends and tendencies of contemporary Canada are not infallible pointers towards its future; but they are the only indications we have got. I'm going to speculate about what lies in store for us Canadians, basing my speculations on the record of our recent past.

A speech given by Professor Creighton on receiving an honorary doctorate at Dalhousie University in 1973. A version of this piece was published in *Maclean's*, under the title "Is Canada more than we can hope for?" in September 1973.

19

It is not necessary, nor is it advisable, for our purpose, to go very far back in time. I am going to take the period from the opening of the Second World War to the present, a period of about thirty years, or a little more. A good many of you here tonight have witnessed the passage of all these three decades: the memories of others go back still further into the past; and even the youngest members of the audience have lived through more than half of this stretch of time. You are all quite familiar with it, particularly with its last five or ten years; and its last five or ten years are, I suggest, very much of a piece with the years that preceded them. The period has, as a whole, its own distinctive character and significance. It began dramatically with the opening of the Second World War; and, although I agree that historians are incurably addicted to imposing artificial and arbitrary divisions on historical time, I still feel convinced that the years 1939-41 form one of the great punctuation marks in human history. The opening of the Second World War set in motion a group of world forces, which either initiated, or renewed and accelerated, the principal trends and tendencies in modern Canadian history. During the quarter century that has elapsed since the conclusion of the war, these trends and tendencies have increasingly gained speed and momentum. Will they continue unchecked and with what results for Canadians, or will they be significantly altered and in what direction? If modern Canadian history is a story of which we have seen the beginning and the middle, what will be the end?

If we are to make conjectures about the prospects of the age in which we live, we must first define what we think are its chief characteristics and trends. It is, I believe, an astonishing period, astonishing in respect of what North America and, indeed, the whole western world, regards as the most significant aspect of contemporary society – its growth. The words growth and development are, indeed, the most mystically potent words in the vocabulary of the twentieth century; and the extraordinary character of Canadian growth during the last decades lay in the fact that it was not confined to the economic sphere, though the advances here were indeed spectacular, but was extended through a wide range of human activities, social, political, intellectual, and artistic. In 1941, Canada was a country of 11.5 million inhabitants; in 1971, their number had increased to 21.5 million. In thirty years, the nation had virtually doubled its population, an achievement which had been reached on only one previous occasion, the period 1901-1931. Two factors – a sustained high birth rate and a vast influx of immigrants, many of them with skilled trades and professions – had once more resulted in an exceptionally rapid population growth. The labour force soon began its swift upward climb; and this immense increase in our human resources was accompanied by an equally valuable expansion of our material resources, and particularly by the discovery of large deposits of the two main modern forms of energy, oil and natural gas.

Industrialization and urbanization moved forward with increasing speed. City and town life became the dominant style of Canadian society. The building of houses, "high-rise" apartments, hotels, shopping plazas, and city-centres, never seemed to catch up with the demand. The network of arrangements by which food, clothes, heat, light, comfort, and convenience were all lavishly made available to Canadians increased steadily in complexity. The airplane and the motor-car took over most of the business of transport; and huge airports, and multiple-lane highways, bordered with garages, service stations, hamburger stands, and motels, appropriated more and more of the countryside. Technology, which created machines as huge as the 747 aircraft and as small as the labour-saving devices in the normal Canadian kitchen, lightened the business of living to an extent which would have seemed miraculous only thirty years before. The average Canadian of the 1960s, it has been calculated, had the benefit of services which, in ancient times, could have been provided only by about four hundred slaves. A king in the heroic age who possessed four hundred slaves would surely have been regarded as a rich monarch; and during the last thirty years, Canada enjoyed a prosperity which grew steadily into affluence and was checked only occasionally by brief recessions.

Before 1939, most of the human benefits of such a prolonged boom would have been monopolized by a lucky minority; but in the thirty years that followed, a revolutionary change occurred in the purposes and functions of the Canadian nation. At the opening of the Second World War, Canada had been primarily a *laissez-faire*, non-interventionist state; but by 1970, its various governments were actively engaged in promoting and encouraging growth, equalizing development throughout the provinces, and redistributing the national income among different classes and regions. They had built up an elaborate social security system, and made comprehensive medical and hospital services available to all at public expense. The scope of higher education was enormously expanded to enable young Canadians to fill the needs and grasp the opportunities of the new technology. Old universities were enlarged, new and imposing universities were quickly constructed; and a generous distribution of government grants made college students out of a large proportion of the young people who were coming to maturity in the early 1960s.

Before the opening of the Second World War, state aid was granted only to research in the physical and biological sciences; now it was made available also to scholarship in the social sciences and the humanities. A new company of poets and novelists, assisted by the Canada Council, grew steadily in number; and the performing arts, theatre, ballet, and opera, where before the war Canada had shown almost no independent initiative at all, were now alive with varied and sophisticated talents.

In nearly all these developments, Canada was simply a microcosm of the western world at large. It differed from other nations chiefly in the fact that it was careering onward at a faster pace than most. Its individuality was apparent, not so much in these economic, social, and cultural aspects of growth, but in its political phase, where Canada was clearly distinctive, if not unique. Its distinction derived chiefly from its history, its federal constitution, from the unusual ethnic composition of its people, and from its complex relationships – economic, social, and political – with the two great English-speaking countries, Great Britain and the United States. Politically, Canada was a constitutional monarchy and a member of the British Commonwealth; ethnically, it was a mixed community, a cultural mosaic. Its constitution had been highly centralized in intention; its ally had always been Great Britain and its hereditary antagonist the United States. All these distinguishing features of the Canadian nation had begun to alter long before 1939; but, with the opening of the Second World War, the pace of change quickened and its scope grew. The trend towards constitutional decentralization, after a brief recovery of federal power during the war, was resumed. Ethnic origin no longer signified mother tongue, and by 1961, over 400,000 French Canadians and 2.5 million New Canadians had adopted English as their first language. The imperial connection was steadily weakened by Canada's separatist policies, and by Great Britain's wartime alliance with the United States, and her growing attraction to the European economic community. At the same time, and by a parallel and complementary process, Canada's links with the United States became so numerous and so powerful that they threatened to convert the nation into a political vassal, an economic tributary, and a cultural colony of the American Empire.

II

These, it seems to me, are the dominant themes and trends in Canadian history during the last three decades. Are they likely to continue substantially unaltered, or will they be modified and changed? In theory a nation might alter the direction of its course for either or both of two main reasons. A drastic transformation in its circumstances might compel change; or it might prefer change in the belief that its existing plans were wrongly chosen, that they had not yielded the hoped-for results and had had unforeseen and unfortunate consequences. There is a good deal of evidence that the Canadians may have to alter the tenor of their ways for both of these reasons; but until very recently they were not prepared to consider even the slightest deviation from the familiar path of growth and progress. Every generation is the mental prisoner of the age in which it lives. Truth for any man, said Spengler, is the picture of the world which was borne at his birth. Canadians were not dissatisfied with the new nation they had created; their leaders grew, in fact, extremely complacent about it. The Speech from the

Throne, in the last session of the old Parliament, spoke of the "just society," as if its establishment in Canada would be a matter of a few months, or a few years at most. Plato conceived an ideal republic in order to discover the meaning of justice, and tried, in vain, to persuade the tyrant of Syracuse to build a just society according to his specifications. He might have had much better luck with Prime Minister Trudeau.

It is highly significant that reference to the "just society" disappeared from the Speech from the Throne in the first session of the new Parliament. The general election [of October 30, 1972] had undeniably revealed not only a lot of sceptical disbelief in the near approach of the "just society," but also a good many dissatisfactions and much disillusionment with things as they actually were. A large number of Canadians were certainly prosperous, well-fed, comfortably housed, with plenty of money for drink, travel, and entertainment. They ought to have been contented; but the truth was they were not. They were nagged by the disquieting suspicion that their apparent affluence was not a reality but a delusion. Why – and this was perhaps the most important reason for their doubt – why was there such a startling discrepancy between the availability of jobs and the supply of money? On the one hand, in September 1972, 632,000 people or 7.1 per cent of the labour force were out of work; but on the other, consumer prices and the cost of living generally were rising with scarcely any interruption. Moreover, these monstrous phenomena were not exchangeable. Efforts to check inflation seemed to produce more unemployment. Attempts to promote employment apparently resulted in more inflation. The fact seemed to be that economic controls and social security had failed, almost as badly as *laissez-faire* and individual enterprise, to cure poverty and expense.

This failure was perhaps the greatest, but by no means the only, crime with which the new system was charged. Like the liberal, individualist regime which it had replaced, it appeared to be guilty of a surprising amount of fraud, corruption, and inequity. All Canadian governments had been busily attempting to promote economic growth by granting tax exemptions, subsidies, and "forgivable loans" – as they were quaintly called in Ontario – to large business corporations. At the same time, all Canadian governments had been engaged with equal zeal in redistributing the national income through all sections and classes of the community by means of pensions, welfare, unemployment insurance, health and other social services. This whole benevolent system, though undoubtedly conceived in heaven, began to acquire a suspiciously familiar and very earthy appearance. Canadians suddenly began to realize that the financial largesse and social security provided by government were open to some very formidable attacks. Mr. Lewis charged that the big corporations or "corporate welfare bums," as he called them, had been given financial help or were exempted from taxation at the expense of the already overburdened individual taxpayer. Other critics of the Liberal government insinuated that it had given its regional subsidies – "goodies," they were frankly called – to politically favoured provinces, such as Quebec. Finally – and this produced the greatest shock of all – Canadians began to recognize that a man or woman could do as well, or nearly as well, or perhaps a little better, on relief or unemployment insurance than on the immediately available job; and that a good many ingenious and indolent Canadians were taking advantage of this attractive opportunity. "Jobless freeloaders" and the "welfare rip-off" became a potent, but not openly acknowledged, issue during the election campaign. A month later, Dr. Reuben Baetz, the Executive Director of the Canadian Council on Social Development, publicly criticized some of the provisions of the Unemployment Insurance Act, pointed out its vulnerability to fraud, of which he gave some telling examples, and predicted that, although professedly an insurance scheme, paid for by premiums, it was likely to cost the taxpayers of Canada over two billion dollars in 1972.

The two billion dollars of public money, which met the gaping deficit in the Unemployment Insurance Fund, was a striking illustration of the fact that Canada's rapid progress had been purchased at enormous cost. Undoubtedly governmental expenditure had its swiftest ascent in the 1960s, with the vast expansion of postsecondary education and the introduction of medicare. The unqualified public belief in the value of more education, and the confident assumption that the need for it would grow annually greater, piled up heavy fixed charges for new buildings and enlarged and better paid staff. The huge demands which the public immediately began to make on free, or nearly free, medical services drove the cost of public health up to alarming heights. All during the 1960s, governments had been generous, even prodigal; they had accepted, even anticipated, public pressure; and federal and provincial personal income tax, a mere 1.4 per cent of the national income in 1939, rose to 12.8 per cent in 1969. Then, with startling abruptness, the brakes were applied. Capital grants to hospitals and universities were sharply curtailed. A sudden and unaccountable shortfall in student enrolment revealed the inadequacy of the per capita grants system. Some university administrators, professors, and a good many students felt simply that they had been betrayed. Doctors contemplated with growing anxiety the prospect of becoming salaried servants of the state.

There were a good many reasons – frauds, abuses, inequities, and costs – for the public disillusionment. Most Canadians assumed that these were temporary maladies which could be cured by a few judicious reforms; but a few saw in them the symptoms of a much more profound and possibly incurable disease in the body of contemporary society. For thirty years, Canadians had been demanding more of everything – more growth, more money, more cars, more roads, more planes, more travels, more services, more comforts and conveniences – with a voracious and insatiable appetite. Now, some of them were beginning to realize the enormous price they were called upon to pay, not only in fraud, expense, political corruption, economic injustice, and arbitrary government action, but also in basic human needs and values, for the monstrous contemporary society they had created. Six years ago, a professor in London University published a book called *The Cost of Economic Growth*. The cover of the paperback edition portrayed a man hanging from a tall gallows which, on closer inspection, turned out to be a stylized drawing of the familiar pound sterling sign. The hanging man is shouting "Help!" Below, another man, in spectacles, perhaps intended as a caricature of the author, replies "As ye grow, so shall ye weep."

There was certainly cause for tears in economic growth, but a good many Canadians instead of indulging in vain weeping, decided to take action. Some, like the students who had inexplicably left college, simply "opted out" – retired early, sold their businesses, left their jobs, and fled to whatever seclusion they could find. Others entered the ranks of the conservationists and environmentalists and joined the fight against the contamination of air and water, the rising crescendo of noise and the spoliation of agricultural and recreational land. Even the most prodigious creations of the growth age – high-rise apartment blocks, multi-lane highways, elevated expressways, huge air terminals – came under attack. The new Minister of Municipal Affairs in British Columbia announced the revolutionary doctrine that cities were for people and not for cars. The provincial government of Ontario began to subsidize public transport. The urban and suburban "developer," once a venerated exemplar of municipal growth, became a hated and execrated figure. A huge new expressway through central Toronto has been cancelled. An even more grandiose prospect – the second Toronto international airport – may suffer the same fate.

III

All these signs of an urge or an inclination to change were confined to economic and social affairs. The indications of any real departure from the established trends in recent political history were fewer in number and much less serious, with one exception. A few voices were raised against the persistent republicanization of Canadian forms and ceremonies; a larger body of very vocal dissenters began to protest against the continual American takeover of Canadian industries and natural resources. This resistance was never very widespread or powerful; and the only really determined effort to change the course of history came with the outbreak of the so-called "Quiet Revolution" in Quebec and its declared aim of resisting assimilation and reasserting French-Canadian cultural autonomy. The federal government, which had paid scant attention to the minor political protests, bent a very attentive and sympathetic ear to what was happening in Quebec. It proclaimed the

27

principle that Canadian Confederation should be developed "on the basis of an equal partnership of the two founding races." It appointed a Royal Commission on Bilingualism and Biculturalism, and set up a constitutional conference for the reform of the British North America Act. In the meantime, as interim measures, Parliament passed the Official Languages Act and the government instituted a vigorous programme for promoting bilingualism in the civil service at Ottawa.

Now, nearly ten years later, it is only too evident that this elaborate campaign has been largely a failure. Its most ambitious achievement, the revision of the British North America Act, embodied in the so-called "Victoria Charter," was rejected out of hand by Quebec, the very province it was mainly designed to satisfy. The Census of 1971 has revealed the disturbing fact that the proportion of Canadians speaking French as their mother tongue had declined since 1961 – after a decade of earnest attempts to encourage its growth – by more than a point to 26.8 per cent. As a result, the federal bilingual districts have been reduced in number; and the resentful unrest of the civil servants has slowed down the promotion of bilingualism in Ottawa. The attempt to create a united bilingual Canada, to give French Canada a more satisfactory place in the life of the nation as a whole, has not succeeded. What has succeeded was that other endeavour – always primary with many French-Canadian leaders – the endeavour to grant Quebec a special and virtually separate place in the Canadian federal system. The pursuit of equal partnership had not in fact increased national unity; it had deepened national divisions. And as a result it inevitably accelerated another important post-war trend in Canadian politics – the decentralization of Canadian Confederation. The federal government had attempted through a series of shared-cost programmes, to maintain the national interest and influence in the social welfare fields which constitutionally belonged to the provinces; but now Quebec, demanding money with no strings attached, claiming exclusive administrative control, led the way out of these joint enterprises. Gradually, Ottawa has been reduced nearly to the level of a tax-collecting agency for a group of independent provinces, some of them veritable kingdoms, which compete for foreign investment, and try to rival each other's economic growth and welfare standards. Increasingly vital Canadian decisions are solved – if they are solved at all – by diplomatic negotiations between governments; and thus the irresponsible federal-provincial conference, and the private meetings of provincial premiers became in effect the real institutions of Canada's national government.

In the absence of any purposeful direction, Canada drifts along on its accustomed post-war course, away from Great Britain and the Commonwealth and closer to the United States. It has no defined national goal of its own. After nearly forty years of vain effort, it has not yet found an acceptable method of performing that basic act of sovereignty, amending its own constitution. Canadians still show, at times, a warm attachment to their monarchical institutions; but with Great Britain's entry into the European Economic Community, the decline of the old Commonwealth relationship is continuing, not seriously lamented and almost unremarked. Canada now stands alone in North America, in immediate proximity to the greatest nation in the world, the nation which, above all others, subscribes most unreservedly to the belief that material progress is the only way to the good life. The voracious demands of the American military machine and the American high standard of living have gradually forced the United States to depend more and more upon Canada's natural resources; and much of Canada's economic growth during the last thirty years has its explanation in the huge exports of raw materials to the Republic. Canadians, themselves, half converted to the belief that economic development is the only sure road to happiness, have grown accustomed to selling out their birthright for a quick buck.

IV

It seems evident from this survey, that there is no clear sign of a decisive impending change in the direction of Canadian society. On the one hand, popular dissatisfaction and impatience with painful consequences of economic growth have undoubtedly been growing; but, on the other, the resistance of established economic and social values, and the inertia of a government, almost in-

29

capable of carrying out a collective agreement, even if one could be made, may prove strong enough to postpone serious change for a long time. Canadians may never reach a reasoned decision about their future; but they may – sooner than they think – have their minds made up for them. They may be compelled, or gradually induced, to alter their way of life by a fundamental change in their circumstances. Two very significant factors in the great Canadian upswing of the past thirty years were a rapid population growth and the exploitation of new industrial materials and sources of energy. Will they still lend their help in sustaining Canada's phenomenal growth? And if their contribution declines in importance, how may Canadian development be affected in the future?

The Canadian birth rate began to drop in 1960, and for the last half-dozen years it has been lower than at any other period during the previous half-century. It will be years, of course, before the recruits for the labour force or post-secondary education show any signs of a decline and longer still before the population growth rate will be affected. Yet this steady and increasingly serious drop over a decade appears to have established a trend – a trend directly the opposite of that which characterized Canadian development since the opening of the Second World War. If it continues for another few decades, this tendency may result in an appreciable change in the composition of the Canadian population, and if it persists long enough it will lead ultimately to its stabilization, apart, of course, from immigration. Nobody can foretell – in this matter perhaps above all others – how long a trend will continue. In the late 1930s, when the birth rate was low, though not so low as it is now, Canadian demographers predicted a very slow population growth, much slower than in fact occurred. The event falsified their prophecies and it may do so again. Yet there are two essential differences between 1939 and now. At the beginning of the Second World War, the whole question of family limitation was still cloaked in secrecy and moral disapproval. Now, effective means of birth control are available and abortion is increasingly condoned and may be legalized.

This slackening in the population growth rate may turn out to be a fundamental change in Canadian circumstances; another, still more portentous, is the depletion of our non-renewable natural resources, particularly oil and natural gas. Along with hydro-electric power, these fuels have provided the energy for much of the economic growth and urban development of the past thirty years. Yet there is a crucial difference between them. Water power annually renews itself; oil and natural gas cannot be renewed, they can only be conserved; but, instead of being conserved, they are, in fact, being squandered in a most spendthrift and prodigal fashion. Canadians are guilty parties to this waste; but they are also next-door neighbours of another people, ten times as numerous as themselves, with vastly greater industrial and transport machinery, and an even greedier appetite for luxurious living. The United States has long since turned to Canada to aug-ment its own diminishing supplies of fuels; and the news that con-fidential talks about a common Canadian-American energy policy are proceeding regularly in Washington is full of sinister meaning for Canadians. The scarcely concealed aim of the American government and people is to convince Canadians that their natural resources, including oil and gas, are really continental resources, freely available to Americans in exactly the same way as their own domestic supplies. Canada, in short, ought to be expendable in the service of the American industrial empire and the American high standard of living.

One doesn't need to be a prophet of gloom and doom to predict that this prodigious consumption of non-renewable energy cannot go on accelerating for ever; and if Canadian resources are to be wasted in the satisfaction of a continent of 300 million extravagant people, the end may come more quickly than we think. It is only twenty-five years since the famous discovery of the Leduc oil field in Alberta, and already the exploitation of our last reserves in the Arctic has begun and the possibilities of the Athabasca tar sands have come under consideration. Man's love affair with the automobile may come to an end simply because for most Cana-dians this mistress will get too expensive to keep; and the effortless warmth of furnaces fired by oil and natural gas may die away for ever. Coal and electric power will remain; nuclear energy may be developed; but the decline in the supply of oil and natural gas will

31

effect a transformation in the basic circumstances of our existence, the extent of which it is almost impossible to imagine. All that we can be certain of is that the consequences will affect Canadians far more seriously than other North Americans. A continental oil policy will produce very unequal results across the continent. For many citizens of the United States, it will simply mean more discomfort, simplicity, and hard work. For many citizens of Canada, it may make life almost insupportable.

Changes, whether we will them or not, are probably on their way. How will Canadians cope with them? They have, it seems to me, two choices. They can start making small adjustments and increasingly painful economies, which will enable them to delay, but not to escape, the inevitable end; or they can begin to plan now for an entirely different manner of existence. For thirty years, they have acted on the principle that economic growth and prosperity was the only road to the good life. Their motto has been "Enough does *not* suffice." Or, to quote the old Indian squaw's opinion of whisky, "A little too much is just enough." The time may come when there will *not* be "a little too much" of everything; but there will be enough, if Canada strives not for growth but equilibrium, if she achieves a stable population, and if she carefully guards most of her natural inheritance, her birthright, and particularly her precious fuels, for this and future generations of Canadians. An indefinite prospect of modest contentment stretches before this country, if only Canadians have the wisdom to ensure it; but this radical change in the direction of their course requires a new conception of the purpose of life, a strong belief in the value of Canadian national independence, and a real capacity for united action by Canadian governments. And all this is perhaps far more than we can hope for.

Surviving in
the Post-Keynesian Era

Only two years ago, the members of the Club of Rome, and the other prophets of an impending crisis in the affairs of man and his world, were still the objects of scorn, ridicule and indignation. Who, it was asked angrily, were these absurd and criminal Cassandras? Why did they think themselves entitled to subject us to such needless and monstrous terrors? They had, it was charged, based their revelations on inadequate and highly questionable information. They had misused that wonderful new electronic device, the computer. Their predictions of the future were exaggerated and grotesque. They were, in fact, preposterously wrong. Mankind was not headed for an abyss. On the contrary, mankind was destined for even higher uplands of affluent and gracious living. The natural resources of the world, while not perhaps exactly inexhaustible, could certainly last, with careful management and conservation, into the indefinite future. Even if, in the very long run, part of man's natural endowment should decline or fail, his powers of invention would respond to the challenge of need and a synthetic substitute, which would be just as good as the original, and probably even better, would be quickly supplied.

Then, in the autumn of 1973, complacency began to seep away. It was not that the human condition and the state of the world had suddenly and dramatically changed; it was simply that changes

---

Published in *Maclean's* as an article entitled "We've Been Fat Too Long and Now It's Too Late," in April 1975.

33

which had been inexorably growing over a number of years became abruptly and startlingly manifest. Man and the enormous industrial machine he has created in modern times have always depended ultimately on ample and cheap supplies of fuel – of food for human beings and energy for their mechanical contrivances. Food and energy had always been available before, in apparently unlimited quantities and at relatively moderate prices, to the industrialized nations of western Europe and North America. They counted on the continuance of these essentials with as much confidence as they counted on the rising of the sun; but they failed to realize that their near-monopoly of the choicest food and the cheapest sources of power was no longer nearly so unquestioned and secure as in the past. Their monopoly had in fact been challenged by other, partly developed and undeveloped nations which believed they knew the secret of the West's success, and were eager to employ modern technology, build up industry, and improve the health and welfare of their peoples.

Humanity as a whole, and not simply a privileged portion of it, now realized the incalculable value of the vital fuels. But the West was still their most voracious consumer, gobbling up larger quantities than ever before; and the crisis began in the autumn and winter of 1973-74 when the western nations suddenly discovered that food and energy had, almost without warning, become scarce and dear. Canada and the United States saw at last the rapid depletion of their own deposits of petroleum. Europe and North America watched with consternation and fury when the primitive countries of the Middle East, which had been selling their one great asset for what the world chose to pay for it, suddenly realized their coercive power over western industry and quadrupled their price for oil. Developing nations, which until very recently had been peasant communities subsisting contentedly on fish and cereals, now began to demand the meat, eggs, and fruit that the citizens of a few wealthy powers had virtually monopolized before. Even cereals, man's first and basic foodstuff for centuries, had become scarce and costly. Vast areas of the earth's surface in eastern Europe, Asia, and Africa, which in the past had always produced enough grain to feed their peoples, with something left over for export, were now obliged to supplement their own crops with supplies from the world's breadbasket, North America. All of a sudden there was famine, scarcities, preposterously high prices, which stoked the fires of inflation and rocked the rickety mechanism of international exchange. The gloomy predictions could no longer be dismissed as nightmarish delusions. The crisis they had foreseen was no longer far off. It was not even impending. It had come.

The bewildered inhabitants of the western world wondered miserably what had befallen them. Their accredited pundits – politicians, economists, statisticians, and journalists – all offered their complicated explanations. But the real explanation was at ·once more basic and simpler. It lay in contemporary man himself, in his grandiose conception of what the world's resources and his own ingenuity could yield him. It was not simply a belief in the indefinite continuance of the rich and easy way of life; it was also, and more importantly, an intimate conviction in an annual, never-failing increment of convenience, comfort, leisure, and entertainment. Material prosperity, it was assumed, would last forever; but it was also expected to grow, a little at the very least, and probably a lot, every year.

The theoretical origins of this golden age are to be found in the doctrines of an economist, John Maynard Keynes, who, in 1936, published a book that transformed the economic theories of the West and revolutionized all western economies. If, as Keynes argued, a nation wished to escape the prolonged distress of a depression, it could buy its way back into recovery; it could lift the levels of employment and income by public and private expenditure.

This new economic evangel quickly captured the minds of the mandarins in the Bank of Canada and the federal Department of Finance after the Second World War. What they feared most was a return of the Depression which had hurt Canada so badly before the Second World War; and their whole post-war programme was conceived with the aim of achieving a high and steady level of employment and national income. The elaborate system of improved social welfare measures which the federal government proposed to the federal-provincial conference in 1945, was designed not only to level out the gross inequalities in Canadian incomes but also to distribute purchasing power as widely as possible. Veteran's benefits, family allowances, old-age pensions and unemployment insurance pay would all put money into the hands of people who could be counted on to spend and keep on spending.

This was the potent elixir that started Canada off on its supposedly endless spree of exuberant life. Years went by, good times continued on their steady way, and gradually high employment and high incomes began to grow familiar, commonplace, even a little unsatisfactory. It was no longer sufficient to avoid depressions and to maintain prosperity. There must be growth, regular and consistent growth! Every government and every corporation in Canada quickly made growth its overriding aim. The possibilities and prospects of growth became the nation's chief concern; quarterly, and then monthly, economic reports became essential to the nation's peace of mind. A significant rise in the gross national product represented the sum of human happiness.

During the 1950s and 1960s, the rapid increase in growthmania did strange things to the Canadian people and their governments. Government was, of course, intended to play a major part in the Keynesian scheme of things; but Canadian governments found it convenient to forget that their role, as Keynes had devised it, was essentially a balancing role. They made hardly any attempts to moderate or stabilize the rate of growth; but they gave their talents eagerly to the business of inspiring and promoting it. Obviously the first duty of a growth-minded government was to grow itself. Soon a highly trained and extremely expensive army of "growthmen" – economic planners, technocrats, promoters, and engineers – began to help the government in concocting its vast expansionary plans. Even the rapidly growing civil service apparently proved incapable of discovering enough urgent needs and inventing enough expensive projects to maintain consistent growth. It became customary to appoint an individual or group – at high rates of pay, of course – to investigate this, or study that, or report on the other. Almost invariably also, it proved necessary to engage another individual or group – and naturally at still bigger fees – to review the report, or reconsider the study, or evaluate the findings of the investigation.

Under the incessant urgings of growthmania, the role of all Canadian governments steadily expanded. The "public sector" – the very phrase would have been almost incomprehensible to the pre-war generations – took over such a mammoth portion of national production that the word "slice" became laughably inappropriate. Through the experience and knowledge they had already acquired, Canadian governments were far better fitted than, for example, American governments, to assume a large share in the control and direction of the economy. Public ownership as an instrument of national expansion had been solidly established before 1939; and now the federal equalization grants, which transferred large sums from the richer to the poorer regions of the country, enabled even small provinces to take a hand in the exciting task of promotion. Federal and provincial governments discovered new and expensive ways of exploiting their resources of petroleum, natural gas, nuclear energy, metals, and water power. They were becoming landlords on a large scale, expropriating large tracts of land for unnecessary airports or satellite towns. Sometimes they competed and sometimes they co-operated with each other in persuading corporations to establish factories in particular localities. Generous subsidies and "forgivable loans" were granted to industries with a nice sense of equitable geographical distribution. Even when the fertile imaginations of politicians, civil servants, and consulting "growth-men" ran out of ideas for new and costly projects, the federal government did not for a minute relax its efforts to lift the level of employment and income. Through the Local Initiatives Program, and the Opportunities For Youth Program, it invited Canadian citizens to concoct their own trivial make-work schemes.

The growth age did strange things to Canadian governments; it did even stranger things to the character of the Canadian people. It didn't seem to matter very much whether the Canadians had religious beliefs, or political convictions, or intellectual interests, or artistic talents. Their only really important attribute was that, somehow, they got money and spent it quickly. Above all else, they were consumers – or rather, not exactly consumers but buyers. Their houses and garages were full of assorted unused junk, which they had never needed, or had discarded and forgotten, or which was now useless because its manufacturer, despite his "lifetime" guarantee, had thoughtfully ensured its rapid obsolescence. If a purchase remained unconsumed or neglected, it was of no consequence; it had been bought and that fulfilled the one real purpose of its creation. The only expenditure which was not considered legitimate was the expenditure of one's own time, skill, and energy. Debt became a chronic condition which every government and every financial institution in the country did its best to popularize. Credit cards, charge accounts, bank loans, instalment purchases all helped Canadians to keep on buying more than they could afford.

It was this craze for spending and borrowing that widened the scope of growthmania until it assumed the proportions of a national epidemic. Governments and corporations had started the organized pursuit of growth; now it was the turn of the populace, a populace habituated to constant buying and forced to live in a world of steadily rising prices.

When the crisis of food and fuel arrived in the autumn of 1973, Canadians at first greeted it with total disbelief. They refused to admit that their thirty-year joyride on the climbing roller coaster of the growth age could ever plunge downward. Other countries – England, Japan, Italy, and even the United States – might be in trouble, but not Canada! It simply couldn't happen here! The prices of oil and gasoline jumped up sharply. There were lines of cars at filling stations in the United States and Europe. There was talk of additional taxes and even of rationing as a means of reducing the wasteful use of motor fuel. These ominous signs made hardly the slightest impression on Canadians. In their view, the idea that one should ever, for any reason, stop buying that glittering symbol of the growth age, the large North American motor-car, was simply too preposterous for words! During 1974, for a whole year after the crisis was well under way, and when every motor-car firm in western Europe and America was facing battalions of unsold cars, Canadians set a record for domestic car and truck sales.

There was at least some justification for their complacency. As Prime Minister Pierre Trudeau and his colleagues kept repeating with tiresome iteration, they were still rather better off than other peoples. Despite very high prices, there was still plenty of food, including the criminally wasteful surplus of 28 million rotten eggs; and Canada's own petroleum deposits partly shielded it against the impact of the huge increase in the world price of oil.

In the short run, the self-satisfaction of the Canadians was justified; but in the long run, it was unwarranted, for it lulled them into a serious miscalculation of the future. Many of the special advantages which sustained self-confidence in 1973-74 were inherently temporary. Canada was a trading nation, most of whose national income was derived from foreign trade, and any serious slump in world commerce would quickly reduce external sales. The United States, moreover, was the nation's best customer, and more than two-thirds of Canadian exports, chiefly natural products, renewable and non-renewable, were consigned to the United States. A depressed United States would certainly buy less of the basic staples than it had during the boom; but the drop in American demand was infinitely less serious than the rapid decline in the Canadian capacity to supply. Canada had, in fact, been selling its birthright to the Americans for thirty hectically prosperous years without a simple thought for the future. The future had now arrived, but it took the energy crisis of 1973-74 to awaken the Canadians to its appalling significance. The depletion of the most easily accessible sources of their most lucrative, non-renewable fuels – petroleum and natural gas – had now gone so far that their total exhaustion was probable in less than a decade. Canada would sell less high-priced energy to the United States for the simple, shattering reason that there would be much less to sell, and still less to export, after the government, rousing itself, but too late, from its criminal credulity and negligence, attempted to save a part of the dwindling residue for Canadians. Never again would Canada's primary industries produce the astonishing bonanza of the growth age. Its secondary industries, which had come so largely under the ownership and control of multinational corporations in the United States, were still more closely united with American manufacturers through special arrangements such as the auto pact; and a depression south of the border was bound inevitably to travel north. Canada was like a spendthrift who had run through his own inheritance and had engaged himself as a permanently indentured servant to a very hard-up master.

What was the Canadian government to do? Had it any real options? Did it even know whether it ought to be fighting inflation or depression? The tenets of Keynesian orthodoxy prescribed rigorous fiscal and monetary restraints during a boom, and deficit budgets, reduced taxation, heavy government expenditures and easy money for a slump. Theoretically these alternative courses of action were still open, but in the baffling contradictory state of affairs produced by thirty years of unparalleled growth there was really no choice at all. Except on one recent occasion, when the Trudeau government had tentatively introduced some restrictions and hastily abandoned them at the first slight sign of increasing unemployment and popular disapproval, traditional economic restraints had never been seriously regarded as possible policies in Canada. In thirty years, the Canadian government had hardly ever employed any but expansionary methods. Now, with the country mired in an acknowledged recession, it was too late to put on the brakes. The only thing to do was to go on spending – and printing – money.

At the end of the Second World War two roads to the future were still open to the Canadian people. They could have opted for economic stability, economic independence, social security, and modest contentment. They could have stopped or drastically limited the American takeover of their native industries. They could have retained ownership and control of their precious fuels, developed them slowly to suit their own needs and purposes, and ensured the comfort and convenience of themselves and their descendants for centuries to come. They did, of course, none of these things. Instead they allowed these non-renewable resources to fall into the hands of the big American multinational companies, which exploited them rapidly with no other thought than their own enrichment and the satisfaction of a continental market grown voracious with industrial growth and affluent living. The only deposits still untouched will be extremely expensive to utilize, either because they are very remote or because they will be difficult to extract. A very grim future awaits the elaborate urban civilization which has grown up in Canada during the past thirty years. Life will be much less easy and comfortable, and decidedly more costly; nothing now can long delay the inevitable approach of the change.

Preserving the Peaceable Kingdom

A few years ago there was published in Toronto a book with the title *Canada: A Guide to the Peaceable Kingdom*. It is a collection of essays, mostly written during the 1960s, about various aspects of Canadian life, and it was edited, with an introduction by a former student of mine, William Kilbourn. I recommend it as a varied and interesting collection; but I am here concerned, not with its contents, but with its title, or rather a part of its title, *The Peaceable Kingdom*. I believe that this phrase "the peaceable kingdom" provides a key to the understanding of Canada, and also that both the adjective "peaceable" and the noun "kingdom" are equally essential and are, indeed, complementary and indivisible parts of a whole. Our Canadian traditions, which we derive from Great Britain, are unique on the continents of North and South America. We have stood for historical continuity rather than revolution, for monarchy rather than republicanism, for parliamentary institutions and responsible government rather than congressional government and constitutional checks and balances. We have tried to promote political stability, social order and personal restraint. We have been ready to limit individual liberty and free enterprise in the interests of public welfare and the general good. Government, law and police preceded, rather than

A speech given by Professor Creighton on receiving an honorary degree from Memorial University of Newfoundland, on October 19, 1974.

followed the Canadian frontier as it travelled across the continent. People can still walk the central streets of the great Canadian cities without fear of injury and molestation; and political assassination has never yet become a hideous blot on Canadian public life.

We do not often reflect on the benefits of our parliamentary institutions and responsible government. We are inclined to take them for granted until we are suddenly reminded, by some dramatic event, of their relative flexibility and efficiency; and naturally these shocking reminders usually occur in countries whose political systems differ radically from our own. It has fallen to the lot of this generation to reach maturity just at the very moment when what is probably the most appalling of all these object lessons – the Watergate scandal in the United States – reached its climax. A long and tangled sequence of intrigue, dissimulation and controversy, which subsided only with the resignation of President Richard Nixon, has injured American government, humiliated the American people, and seriously damaged the prestige of the United States as the principal leader of the western world. It is shocking that such an immense disruption could have taken place in such an old and apparently settled political system; it is even more astonishing, particularly to citizens of parliamentary democracies such as Canada, that it lasted as long as it did. It went on and on, through one revelation, accusation, and denial after another simply because it could be ended only in one of three crucial ways, by the death, impeachment, or resignation of the President.

This was precisely the political impasse which the Fathers of Canadian Confederation sought to avoid. Ignorant Canadians sometimes assume that the Fathers maintained constitutional monarchy and parliamentary government simply because they could not escape from the prison of colonial habit, and the moral pressure of the British government. The facts are, of course, that these basic constitutional decisions were not only the free choice, but also the *deliberate* and reasoned choice of the Fathers, who reached their conclusions only through a detailed knowledge and careful study of other, rival political systems, particularly those on the North American continent. "A great evil in the United States,"

John A. Macdonald said at the opening of the Quebec Conference in 1864, "is that the President is a despot for four years. He is never considered as being the father of his people . . . he is the leader of a party." Both Macdonald and Cartier disliked the uneasy and potentially antagonistic relationship of Congress and Presidency. In their eyes, the constitutional checks and balances which governed this relationship seemed dangerously rigid; and they greatly preferred the British and Canadian system, with the ministry responsible to Parliament. "Our constitution" – and I quote John A. Macdonald again – "should be a mere skeleton and framework that would not bind us down." This political flexibility, which the Fathers of Confederation prized so highly, has certainly saved us from crises so prolonged and shameless as Watergate. The only Canadian scandal, which, without being nearly so infamous, aroused a comparable revulsion in the electorate, was, of course, the notorious Pacific Scandal, which occurred just a little over a hundred years ago. The full revelation of the details of the scandal came in the summer of 1873. Parliament met in October, much earlier than usual as a result of the scandal, and within less than two weeks the Macdonald ministry had resigned.

I have emphasized two principal features of the "peaceable kingdom" – its political stability and its social peace and order. The French and the Americans founded their republics on the social contract and the rights of man – "life, liberty, and the pursuit of happiness," or "liberty, property, security, and resistance to oppression." Our Parliament is empowered simply to legislate for "the peace, order, and good government" of Canada. This is a characteristic Canadian commission, understated and down to earth, rather than rhetorical and idealistic; but however simple and practical our aims have been, they are far more difficult to realize now than they were over a hundred years ago, when the Canadian union was first formed. The Canada that has grown up since the Second World War is much less socially and culturally homogeneous than it was in the nineteenth century and far more politically disunited than the Fathers of Confederation ever expected it would be. There is a bitter irony in the fact that the British North America Act of 1867, which was expressly designed by the Fathers to avoid the dangerous weaknesses of American political decentralization, should have ended up by becoming much more decentralized than the constitution of the United States. Back in the early 1860s, when Canadians were discussing their projected federal union, the American Civil War appeared to most Canadians to be a hideous object lesson of the perils of "states' rights." Now, over a hundred years later, the Canadian provinces, as a result of favourable judicial decisions and aggressive provincial administrations, have gained a far more important place in Canada than the states have ever enjoyed in the American Republic.

Those ten powerful provinces can, and sometimes do, weaken the unity of the "peaceable kingdom"; but they are not the only divisions that perplex its course and threaten its survival. The co-existence of the two different cultures, English-speaking and French-speaking, goes back, of course, to the conquest in 1760; but the twentieth century, and particularly the thirty years since the Second World War, have brought about a strange and complicated variety of divisions and subdivisions in Canadian society. It sometimes seems nowadays as if the "peaceable kingdom" may dissolve into a struggling heap of minorities, big or little in size, racial, cultural or even sexual in character, which organize themselves as pressure groups, thrust themselves into public notice, and demand recognition and special favours from government. This militant assertiveness has gone very far in recent years; it went so far in the Province of Quebec during the 1960s that for a few years a number of thoughtful Canadians began to wonder whether their country was on the eve of dissolution.

These inward divisions are dangerously serious, but equally important is the pressure from without. And Canada's tragic misfortune lies in the fact that during the last thirty years, her growing internal weakness has coincided with the steadily mounting influence of the United States on every aspect of her national life. Since the Second World War, while Canadians have been steadily selling their birthright in order to live in affluence, Canada has taken on more and more of the characteristics of a branch-plant economy and a branch-plant state of mind. The overwhelming majority control of a great and steadily increasing list of major Canadian industries has now passed into the hands of huge international corporations whose headquarters are in the United States. American publishers, books and periodicals, American cinema, radio and television mould and dominate our interests, our ideas, our moral and cultural values. We are ignorant of our history, ill-informed about our own institutions, unaware of our own achievements, neglectful of our scholars, authors, and artists. A questionnaire addressed early this year to students in their final year at High School or Collegiate Institute in the Vancouver region, produced some appalling illustrations of this ignorance and indifference. Seventy per cent of the students could not identify the British North America Act as Canada's written constitution; most of them answered the Declaration of Independence or Magna Carta. Nineteen per cent could not name the capital city of Canada; 23 per cent did not know that Sir John A. Macdonald was Canada's first Prime Minister; 38 per cent were unable to identify the present Leader of the Opposition in the Canadian House of Commons; and 61 per cent could not name *any* three Canadian authors living or dead! And these are students in their last year of secondary school education in a great and wealthy Canadian city!

I believe that Canada, in its headlong rush into continentalism, has very nearly reached the point of no return. If Canadian independence can still be preserved ours is the last generation that can save it. We may ask, of course, how is it possible for people like ourselves, without financial power or influence, to arrest the American takeover of Canadian industry and natural resources; but the time may come, sooner than we may suspect, when we will have the power, if we still possess the will, to use it. And in the meantime, we can inform ourselves and our children about Canada, its resources, its institutions, its public affairs, its art and literature. For if we Canadians ever lose our sense of identity and purpose, we will have lost everything. And then there will be no need for Professor Kilbourn's *Guide to the Peaceable Kingdom*, for the "peaceable kingdom" will have ceased to exist.

Beyond the Referendum

For years, ever since the federal Liberals won power in 1963, English Canada has put its time, its money, its liberal instincts and its genuine goodwill into a prolonged attempt to conciliate Quebec; and now all its efforts have been decisively and contemptuously rejected by the very people they were designed to benefit. A very well-defined period in Canadian history has come to an abrupt end. There is little point now in waiting for the results of René Lévesque's promised referendum. If Quebec's language bill is enacted in its present form, Quebec will legally, as well as morally, have declared its independence. And, if English Canadians wish to defend their country against division and possible ruin, they must devise very different policies, and develop a far more positive attitude to their own future.

For a long time now, the urgent need of a drastic change in English Canada's approach to the enigma of Quebec has been evident; but English Canadians have persistently refused to recognize this necessity, and even the revolutionary events of the past six months have scarcely altered their traditional ways of thinking. Certainly the victory of the Parti Québécois in the Quebec provincial election of November 15, 1976, sent a thrill of consternation and alarm through English-speaking Canada. The shock was profound and terrifying, but its force began fairly quickly to decline, for several reasons. Separatism had not been a principal issue in

---

Published in *Maclean's* as an article entitled "No More Concessions," on June 27, 1977.

47

the election campaign; the Parti Québécois had promised that it would not attempt to secede until a provincial referendum had given it authority to do so; and a public opinion poll, held at the same time as the election, seemed to prove that only a small minority of Quebeckers then favoured secession. These facts did not quiet all English-Canadian fears, but they at least enabled English Canada to recover from its initial panic. At first Lévesque's victory had seemed to imply the inevitable dismemberment of Confederation; but gradually it began to appear, not as a uniquely dangerous threat but simply as a typical incident – though admittedly more alarming than most – in the history of Quebec's relations with the rest of Canada.

For thirty-three years, ever since Maurice Duplessis had regained power in 1944, Quebec has been playing the politics of blackmail. It has played this dangerous game with conspicuous success, for it enjoyed exceptional powers of intimidation and coercion. The solid phalanx of Liberal MPs from Quebec had long been the mainstay of the federal Liberal Party; and for an astounding total of twenty-six years out of the thirty-three, the Liberals had been a power in Ottawa. There were several periods, moreover, during this long stretch of time when they ruled as a minority or with a slim majority, and then they had been particularly vulnerable to pressure. French Canada, represented both by the government of Quebec and the French-Canadian contingent in parliament, had taken advantage of this federal weakness and its own commanding position to promote separate and exclusive French-Canadian interests. It had sought to carry out two main purposes: first, to spread the use of the French language and improve the status of French Canadians throughout Canada; and second, to magnify and glorify the autonomy of Quebec.

The response of English Canada to this calculated pressure might easily have been predicted. English Canada acted as the unsuspecting victims of intimidation have always acted: it tried to meet the politics of blackmail with the politics of appeasement. This meant, in general, that the concept of French Canada as a distinct and separate community must always be allowed to prevail over the idea of Canada as a nation. Canadians were permitted to act together and identify themselves collectively only at times and in ways that French Canada condescended to approve. The postwar project of a Canadian flag, abandoned in 1946 as a result of French-Canadian pressure, was successfully revived, after an interval of nearly twenty years, and only because the Union Jack had been removed from the design. The joint federal-provincial programmes, which Ottawa had attempted to establish after the Second World War, were all gradually abandoned. Quebec refused to accept federal leadership in carrying out national plans and in maintaining national standards. All it wanted from Ottawa was money.

The failure of all attempts to transfer the amendment of the Canadian Constitution from England to Canada is the supreme example of French Canada's successful determination to prevent Canada from becoming a nation and to perpetuate its colonial status. Constitutionally, Canada stood in an abject and humiliating position. Alone of all the nations, big and little, in the western world, it was incapable of amending its own constitution within its own boundaries. Two ministers of justice, the Conservative Davie Fulton and the Liberal Guy Favreau, together devised an amending formula that would have ensured the nation's right to constitutional self-determination. Quebec vetoed it. It even vetoed the so-called Victoria Charter of 1971, that supreme act of English-Canadian generosity and self-abasement, even though it gave Quebec a permanent stranglehold, not only on the amending process but also on major Canadian institutions.

Quebec had succeeded in preventing Canada from achieving its constitutional independence; now it began to question and deny the basically political character of Confederation. The process began with the triumph of Jean Lesage in 1960, and the beginnings of the Quiet Revolution. Canada, the "quiet revolutionaries" announced, was not primarily a political union of a number of different provinces, but a cultural compact between two ethnic communities, French Canadians on the one hand and English Canadians on the other. The essence of Canada was thus its bilingualism and biculturalism, and therefore the paramount task of Canadian governments must be to make these essential elements explicit in both the law and custom of the country.

In the politics of blackmail, this was the ultimate turn of the screw. The bicultural compact theory of Confederation implied drastic and perhaps revolutionary changes. Obviously there were only two main ways in which the aims of the "quiet revolutionaries" could be achieved. The first was an officially bilingual, bicultural but still united Canada; the second was an independent Quebec. For English Canada, there was, of course, no real choice at all. English Canadians had put a century of thought and effort into building a transcontinental nation; and they realized that if its political dismemberment could be prevented only by making major cultural concessions then major cultural concessions would have to be made. It was, as anybody could have foretold, and as everybody will eventually admit, an impossible task, but a gallant attempt was made to carry it out.

In 1963, Prime Minister Pearson established a Royal Commission on Bilingualism and Biculturalism and empowered it to recommend ways in which Canadian Confederation could be developed "on the basis of an equal partnership of the two founding races." The wholesale revision of the language clause, Section 133 in the British North America Act, which the commission recommended in order to extend the legal limits of bilingualism, failed for the simple reason that the Province of Quebec vetoed it. Despite this crushing disappointment, parliament tried to carry out as many of the commission's recommendations as it was constitutionally capable of doing. It passed the Official Languages Act which established federal bilingual districts wherever the minority official language was equal to, or more than 10 per cent of the population. It appointed a Commissioner of Official Languages and began an officious attempt to promote bilingualism in the federal civil service. The English-speaking provinces, impressed by all this federal busyness, started to enlarge the place of French in their educational systems.

The results were certainly mixed and doubtful. Bilingualism in the federal civil service cost vast amounts of money, produced negligible results, and aroused angry resentment among English-speaking bureaucrats. The office of the Commissioner of Official Languages was soon crowded with a robust army of dedicated snoopers, and the commissioner [Keith Spicer, who retired on July 31, 1977] himself appeared to think that his most important public duty lay in abusing and hectoring English Canadians for their neglect of a language only an infinitesimal minority would ever have occasion to use. The bilingual colleges had a tendency to remain only theoretically bilingual; and the French "total immersion" courses in the schools did little more than deepen the illiteracy in English with which pupils tried to enter the universities.

All this English Canadians accepted and endured in the hope that it would help to convince French Canadians that their cultural aims could be realized inside Confederation, and to persuade them to drop the idea of an independent Quebec. They knew, of course, that there were separatists who totally rejected the idea of a bilingual, bicultural nation; but it was not until 1968, when René Lévesque's Parti Québécois emerged as the dominant group in a welter of separatist splinter parties, that the aim of independence seemed to become a real political threat. In the two Quebec provincial elections of 1970 and 1973, the Parti Québécois gained a creditable percentage of the popular vote, but failed to win more than a handful of seats in the National Assembly. Inevitably, Lévesque's victory in November 1976, came with all the staggering shock of the unforeseen and the unexpected.

For a terrifying moment – but for not much more than a moment – English Canadians saw in Lévesque's victory the doom of Confederation. Very quickly they recovered from their first frantic fears. In Canadian politics, they recalled, there were no tragic finalities; there were only endless repetitions of the same themes. The triumph of the Parti Québécois was simply one more extremely savage twist of French Canada's politics of blackmail. It could be successfully met and overcome by one more supreme effort of the politics of appeasement. Almost at once everybody sat back and relaxed in the earnest but complacent attitudes of the 1960s. All the dog-eared plans, the stale proposals and the worn-out, ineffectual remedies were trotted out again as if they sparkled with originality.

Some thought a few "changes" or "adjustments" would be enough to save Confederation. Others, including bank president

W. Earle McLaughlin – bank presidents are now the acknowledged gurus of Canadian public affairs – believed that an entirely new Constitution was necessary. Increasingly, one had the sensation that one was watching the repetition of an old, and very familiar, third-rate television programme. In 1967, John Robarts, then premier of Ontario, held a splendid and extremely costly "Confederation of Tomorrow" conference in Toronto. Now, ten years later, the President of York University has announced, no doubt with Premier Davis's approval, what amounts to another "Confederation of Tomorrow" conference. It is highly probable that not one of these three great public figures has – or had – any clear and definite ideas about what form the Confederation of Tomorrow should take. But that small defect didn't injure the conference of 1967, and certainly it won't impair the success of the conference of 1977. All the delegates will drink a lot, eat a lot, talk a lot; and they will go away with the complacent feeling that they have saved Confederation.

This kind of amiable, well-intentioned, futile talk might have gone on indefinitely. English Canadians thought they had lots of time. They expected that the Parti Québécois would make no decisive move until the results of its promised referendum on independence were known. Their alarm and consternation were all the greater when they suddenly realized that Levesque had no intention of waiting so long. On Friday, April 1 – April Fool's Day – there was tabled in the National Assembly a white paper which described in detail the language policies the Parti Québécois proposed to follow. Quebec, the white paper firmly announced, would henceforth be a unilingual province. "There will be no longer any question of a bilingual Quebec." In future, French was to be the language of government, both central and local, of the courts, of industry, labour and commerce, of education and communications, of place names, street names, and advertisements.

We now know exactly what the Parti Québécois wants and intends to do, and obviously its intentions are unconstitutional. Its language policies repudiate the whole federal bilingual programme and its principal expression, the Official Languages Act. They also defy – which is constitutionally much more serious – Section 133 of the British North America Act, which gives both English and French equal, official standing in the legislature and courts of Quebec. The language rights of the English-speaking minority can, of course, be protected by constitutional methods. Of course, Bill One, the new language proposal, could be disallowed by the federal government or declared invalid by the courts. But Camille Laurin, Quebec's Minister of Cultural Development, has truculently announced that Quebec will pay no attention whatever to executive veto or judicial rejection. Morally, the Parti Québécois is already a revolutionary body.

Unless drastic changes are made before Bill One becomes law, the politics of appeasement will have become totally bankrupt; the policies of self-defence and self-preservation must take their place. There can be no doubt whatever that English Canada desires to survive as a distinct people. Though the proportion may differ slightly from province to province, English Canadians throughout the nation are strongly in favour of preserving Confederation. It is, in fact, very largely their own creation; and the independence of Quebec will unquestionably leave a great, gaping hole in the national structure they have built. If they accept this passively – as they seem at the moment to be doing – it may very well mean the disintegration and disappearance of Canada. If they meet it resolutely they could ensure the survival of a viable and successful nation. They must act at once, and there can only be one resolute approach to the impending fact of separation. English Canadians must quickly decide on the terms on which *alone* they will accept the independence of Quebec. They have foolishly allowed the separatists to take the initiative and to propose terms of their own, terms, of course, devised exclusively in the interest of separation. These must be instantly and uncompromisingly rejected. It is the territorial survival and economic prosperity of Canada to which English Canadians must now devote themselves exclusively. And these are the four major terms on which English Canada would do well to insist:

Boundaries. In the first place, English Canada should accept separation only if Quebec leaves Confederation as it entered it, with exactly the same boundaries that it had in 1867 – minus, of course, the territory of Labrador, which was awarded to Newfoundland by the Privy Council's decision of 1927. In 1867, the vast northern territory, later called the District of Ungava, was not included in the original Province of Quebec. It formed part of Rupert's Land, the chartered territories of the Hudson's Bay Company; and it was not until 1870, three years later, that these territories were bought and paid for by the government of Canada. Ungava remained a part of the Northwest Territories of Canada for more than forty years. The Canadian government granted part of it to Quebec in 1898 and the remainder in 1912. In those days, Quebec was a province of Canada in good standing. If it ceases to be a province of Canada and becomes an independent republic, it can have no moral claim whatever to territories that were essentially gifts of the people of Canada.

The St. Lawrence Seaway. The seaway, which serves Ontario and half a dozen populous states on the American side of the boundary line, is based on a treaty of navigation between Canada and the United States, in which Quebec had no part whatever. The seaway is vital to the prosperity of many millions of people; and, if Quebec secedes, it will acquire a still greater importance as the essential link between Ontario and the Atlantic provinces. Canada must not surrender a single one of its rights and obligations under the treaty; and there can be no doubt that the United States will be just as determined as Canada to insist that the operation of the seaway must remain in their joint and exclusive control. It will probably be necessary to establish a protective zone, under Canadian-American management, on both sides of the seaway. The Panama Canal Zone extends for five miles on either side of the canal; but, in this case, a mile on each side would probably be sufficient.

Language. Since Quebec has rejected bilingualism for unilingualism, English Canada's whole bilingual programme, which never had any constitutional or cultural justification, has ceased to have any political purpose. Unlike Quebec, the English-speaking provinces are under no legal obligation to give English and French equal official status; and whereas the English-speaking minority in Quebec amounted in 1971 to 13.1 per cent of the population, the French-speaking minority totalled less than half that percentage in

Ontario and Manitoba, less than 4 per cent in Saskatchewan, less than 3 per cent in Alberta and less than 2 per cent in British Columbia. Canada should repeal the Official Languages Act, abolish the office of the Commissioner of Official Languages, and cease all efforts to promote bilingualism in the civil service. The provinces – and particularly Ontario – that have been promoting French in the schools for purely political purposes should realize that these purposes are now politically meaningless.

Economic Association. English Canada must make it perfectly clear that neither before nor after separation will it negotiate a customs union with secessionist Quebec. There is something peculiarly offensive in the calm assumption of the leaders of the Parti Québécois that Quebec should be able at one and the same time to enjoy all the political liberties of independence and all the economic advantages of union. Why should English Canadians give the slightest economic advantage to a province that calmly proposes to divide their country and threaten its survival? The Parti Québécois assumes that Quebec and English Canada need each other economically. The truth is, of course, that while Quebec is undoubtedly dependent on English Canada, English Canada could get along very well without Quebec. Once it imposes its tariff along the boundary of the secessionist province, the flight of industry, banking, finance, and labour from Quebec, which has already assumed large proportions, will be magnified and accelerated. And René Lévesque, his associates, and his deluded followers will be left to themselves in the stagnant economic backwater of independence.

The Politics of Pickering

On March 2, 1972, the Governments of Canada and Ontario, like two great eagles sailing high in the sky, swooped down and pounced on the unsuspecting and unprotected citizens of Pickering Township, Ontario County.

A second international airport for the Toronto-centred region, the federal government declared in a joint announcement, will be located in Pickering Township, just to the northeast of Toronto. There had been no warning of this extraordinary czarist ukase.

There had been no public investigation of the question of air transport in the Toronto-centred region. There had not even been the slightest, most perfunctory recognition of that precious principle of "participatory democracy," about which our politicians expatiate so self-righteously when they want our votes.

The arbitrary ordinance of March 2, was, in fact, preceded by nearly three years of almost total silence on the subject of the airport – three years of blessed governmental immunity from the questions and criticisms of the citizens, during which federal and provincial officers, like so many furtive inquiry agents, carried out their secret examinations of possible airport sites.

This policy of concealment was prompted by the early realization that the safest way of settling the question of air transport in southern Ontario was to keep its potential users completely in the dark. At the beginning, of course, there seemed no need for

---

Published in *The Globe and Mail*, headlined "The Grand Outrage of the Grand Old Man," on October 21, 1972.

secrecy, since there was no serious thought of a second international airport for the Toronto region.

The federal government accepted and published the report of its chosen firm of consultants, which recommended that "the expansion of the present Toronto International Airport was the most economic and viable" solution to the problem of increased air traffic in the Toronto area.

This decision, which protected the environment of southern Ontario by the effective method of confining the disturbance of air transport to the terminal in which it had been concentrated for the past quarter-century, was the wisest decision that could have been taken, from every point of view.

But the federal government then proceeded to consult the municipalities and citizen groups which represented the populous community that had grown up around the village of Malton in the past twenty-five years.

The people of this region had voluntarily made their homes there in the full knowledge that an airport existed in their midst and was certain to develop and expand; but they now arbitrarily insisted that it must not grow any further. The federal government accepted their protest. It agreed that "land use compatibility" could not be satisfied if Malton were enlarged, and gave up the idea of expansion. This, the government announced, "is the kind of solution that can emerge when all citizens participate in a dialogue with the Government in a spirit of reason and goodwill."

These pious sentiments most surely have been uttered with tongue in cheek. The federal government had learned its lesson. There must be no more announcements of intention concerning a second Toronto-centred airport. Above all there must be no more consultation with local municipalities and no more dialogue with interested citizens.

From then on, so far as the public was aware, the whole project of the airport was wrapped in silence; but behind this blank wall of official dumbness, the federal and provincial governments were in fact carrying on surreptitious but elaborate surveys, costing millions of dollars, of a wide variety of possible sites, numbering nearly sixty in all, but not including Pickering.

Finally, they narrowed this total to a short list of four; but unfortunately the news of this selection leaked and the citizens of the regions affected promptly protested.

Once again, the federal and provincial governments drew back. Once again, their experts evaluated the Malton terminal and in September 1970, came to the conclusion that its expansion was the best solution to the problem. Once again, the governments at Ottawa and Toronto decided not to follow this advice. From then on, the airport project became top secret.

At last, after eighteen more months of silence and secrecy, the federal and provincial administrations pounced on the Pickering site, a site which had not even been studied in the original massive investigation and had, in fact, never been mentioned before.

No more cynical evasion of the democratic process and no more harsh denial of "participatory democracy" can be conceived. A little more than two years earlier, the federal government had sanctimoniously extolled "the kind of solution that can emerge when all citizens participate in a dialogue with the Government in a spirit of reason and goodwill." Now it deliberately repudiated its own professed principle – a principle that other governments, not so addicted to hypocritical moralizing as the Canadian administrations, have scrupulously honoured.

In the United States, the National Environmental Protection Act requires a public hearing before an enterprise such as the second Toronto airport can be undertaken. In England, the Roskill Commission, set up to advise the British government on the timing and siting of the third London airport, held public hearings at each of the four sites on its short list, as well as at London.

The Canadian Minister of Transport feebly tried to excuse his failure to follow these excellent examples by explaining that he would have loved to have the public participate in the decision-making process, but that he was concerned about the dreadful possibility of speculation in land.

Other countries seem ready to face these terrors in the public interest; and the Minister of Transport himself had listened to the protests of the four communities on his short list, Orangeville, Scugog, Lake Simcoe, and Guelph. Pickering alone was denied the opportunity of presenting its case to the government.

The truth seems to be that the Minister of Transport was sick and tired of "participatory democracy" in the airport issue and was determined to prevent any more of it.

The secretive method by which the governments reached their decision to build the second airport at Pickering was wrong. The decision itself was equally invalid. Long-range forecasting of air traffic is about as exact a science as astrology. Planners are always optimistically predicting an annual growth rate of 10 per cent or 12 per cent; but less than a month ago, the Director-General of the International Air Transport Association gloomily reported that the world airline industry had for the second year in succession suffered a net loss as a result of declining loads and an over-capacity of aircraft.

The reliability of forecasts rapidly diminishes with the increasing length of the time frame; and, when the Canadian government, in an attempt to justify the building of a second airport, estimated that Malton would have to serve 60 million passengers in the year 2000, it had ascended into the stratosphere of visionary speculation. The projection of current trends so far into the future is nothing more than an exercise in technical humbug; but if the time span is reduced to ten or fifteen years, forecasts may approach closer to future reality.

Within these sensible limits the case for a second Toronto airport is extremely weak. In comparison with the traffic growth trends of eleven major North American airports projected down to 1980 Toronto makes a very poor showing, standing in ninth place, with only Montreal and New Orleans below it.

Yet only three of these leading centres – New York, Chicago, and Washington – have experimented with a second airport and in only one, New York, serving 20 million people, has the experiment partially succeeded. In Washington it was a failure and in Chicago a humiliation.

On what basis can two airports, both serving the same area, split the market between them? The airlines are strongly opposed to duplicating their equipment and services at two nearby terminals. The travelling public wants to go where it gets the most comprehensive selection of airline companies and flights.

The fact is that the decision to build a second airport for the Toronto region was not, in any rigorous sense, a planning decision at all. It was, fundamentally, a political decision. For the federal government, it was the almost unavoidable counterpart of another political decision, the decision to build a second major Montreal airport at Ste. Scholastique.

Anyone who has walked through the empty and echoing corridors of Dorval Airport, or travelled along the moving walkway with only a solitary passenger approaching on the other side, may well wonder why a second international airport was needed for the City of Montreal. If he is a Canadian, his wonderment will cease when he remembers that for the past ten years the propitiation of Quebec has become perhaps the basic imperative of Canadian politics.

Unemployment, inflation, foreign ownership, the balance of payments, the economic growth rate, the social service "rip-off," may all cause Ottawa deep concern, though temporary concern, but the appeasement of Quebec has become its uninterrupted and enduring anxiety.

At long intervals, the federal government lifts its gaze from the contemplation of this absorbing problem and recalls the fact that Ontario, with its large population, faster growth rate and stronger industrial and financial base, also exists and is actually, like Quebec, a part of Canada. On such occasions, it is apt to decide that Ontario should be given some obvious *quid pro quo* in the hopes that it will subside and be quiet.

Montreal has been awarded a second airport at Ste. Scholastique. Therefore Toronto ought to have its equivalent at Pickering.

The provincial government's decision to support the construction of a second airport east of Toronto was also governed in large part by politics, but its political reasons differed widely from those of the federal government. One of its main purposes was to promote the development of the eastern part of the province. This was a legitimate, in fact, a worthy object, but the assumption that a second international airport in Pickering was a good way of attaining it could only have resulted from some very muddled – or very devious – thinking.

If the new airport was to have any effect at all on the lower Lake

60

Ontario and the Upper St. Lawrence valley, it would have to be placed far east of Pickering, in an area which could not conceivably produce enough traffic to support it. Sited in Pickering Township, it could exert only a partial and indirect influence even on Oshawa, and virtually none at all on the development of the towns a little farther to the east and north, such as Port Hope, Cobourg and Peterborough. The real beneficiary – or the real victim – of the proposed Pickering airport would be Toronto.

The huge inevitable access highways to the new airport and the construction of the adjacent town of Cedarwood would simply hasten Toronto's hideous urban sprawl. The claim that Pickering airport would promote the growth of eastern Ontario is either a silly delusion or a specious fraud.

Political decisions are socially bad decisions because they are designed mainly to benefit governments in power. If they do serve the public interest it is, in most cases, accidentally or incidentally; and very often, as with the Pickering airport, they may inflict serious injury or irreparable havoc upon the community. From every point of view, the choice of the Pickering site was wrong.

Air navigation will have to face the hazards of Pickering's heavy snows and frequent fogs; geese, ducks, and gulls, which use the area as a flyway, will be frightened away. Above all, nearly 125,000 acres – four-fifths the area of Metropolitan Toronto – of Ontario's Class I agricultural land will be involved in the project.

The airport itself will occupy 18,000 acres; the adjacent Cedarwood community will extend over another 25,000; and finally, vast tracts of land surrounding the airport, the "high-noise areas," as they are bluntly called, totalling about 80,000 acres, will be "frozen" so far as their land use is concerned.

To say that this is some of the very best agricultural land in the province is an economic fact but a serious cultural understatement. The Pickering area is, in fact, very nearly unique. It is one of the last, still relatively unspoiled survivals of the old, lovely countryside of south-central Ontario. The Government of Ontario itself recognized this vital fact when, little more than two years ago, in May 1970, it published, with official approval, the Toronto-

Centred Region Plan. Zone II of that plan, which included much of Pickering Township, was to be reserved for agriculture, conservation, and recreation.

By espousing the project of the Pickering airport, the provincial government has not only abandoned its own sound regional scheme, it has betrayed and destroyed it. It has helped to ensure that the dreadful industrial jungle of steel and brick and glass and concrete, the stupefying nightmare of fumes and filth and noise will extend unbroken all the way around Lake Ontario from Oshawa to Niagara.

Perhaps the most appalling feature of this prospective spoliation and wreckage is that it is not needed. The Pickering airport would not even serve the purpose for which it was supposedly designed.

Only 3 per cent of the traffic at Malton, so government studies indicate, originates from east of Metropolitan Toronto. The vast majority of passengers at the present Toronto airport are drawn – and will continue to be drawn – from the four or five million people who inhabit Toronto and the area to the west. This huge number of potential air travellers would be far more efficiently and conveniently accommodated by an airport sited at Ontario's provincial centre of gravity, just west of Toronto.

The Pickering airport could never satisfy these obvious and compelling requirements. The existing airport at Malton has done so, and can continue to do so, if the plan recommended by the federal and provincial experts in 1967 and 1970 is carried out. Malton, with no enlargement in area, with a single new runway and improved passenger facilities, could continue to give satisfactory service for the foreseeable future. In the meantime, the two governments and the citizens concerned could carry out a comprehensive, detailed and open investigation of the problems of air transport in the Toronto region.

All these considerations ought to have induced the federal and provincial governments to hesitate before they suddenly pounced on Pickering. The fact that they went ahead without consulting, or even informing, the people who would be directly affected by this violent upheaval in the life of the township outraged a number of its residents; and their immediate response, made on March 3, the day after the governments' announcement, was to set up a citizens' organization, People or Planes, to defend their interests.

POP's first aim was to present its case against the second airport before an open forum, and for this it sought to persuade the federal government to grant a formal inquiry under the Public Enquiries Act.

Up to that point, the government had acted bluntly and arbitrarily; now it began to move in an evasive, equivocal and contradictory fashion. Outwardly, it seemed to concede an inquiry – but an inquiry which so completely defeated all the aims of the petitioners that it might have been disingenuously framed for that very purpose.

It was not to be a formal inquiry under the Public Enquiries Act; it was not to concern itself specifically with the Pickering airport, but with transport generally in southern Ontario. Finally, by a grotesque contradiction, which might have convinced the members of POP that they were dealing with either a group of certifiable lunatics or a gang of blatant imposters who didn't even attempt to conceal their fraud, the government announced that it would begin the expropriation of the Pickering properties without waiting for the findings of the inquiry!

For a while it hesitated to carry out this astonishing threat, but recently the formal announcement was gazetted and notices of expropriation have been sent out.

The federal and provincial governments share – in proportions which are unknown to the public – the blame for the accumulated injustice and unwisdom of the proposed Pickering airport.

The provincial government is apparently deaf to appeal and, with three years of power to run, it is also safe from immediate retaliation.

The federal government, fortunately for Canadian voters, is very differently placed. With a general election coming on immediately, it is vulnerable, and from it Canadians can really exact retribution. They can defeat its members in the constituencies, they can weaken or perhaps overthrow the government itself.

A severe electoral shock would be a very suitable retort to the insolent quip which Prime Minister Pierre Trudeau addressed to a puzzled and anxious voter in the Pickering region who wanted to know "Just where I stand." "There is no doubt where you stand," Mr. Trudeau answered with brutal candour. "You are standing on ground that is going to be expropriated."

An appropriate rejoinder springs naturally to the mind: "There is no doubt about the office you are occupying, Mr. Trudeau, and we hope it will be expropriated in nine days' time."

Wine, Spirits, and
Provincial Politicians

A short while ago, Darcy McKeough, the Provincial Treasurer, made a suggestion which seems to have received far less attention than it deserves. Mr. McKeough pointed out that the provincial government had recently become involved in a good many activities which, a generation or so earlier, would have been left in private hands; and he proposed that some of these, including the sale of wine and spirits, might possibly be transferred from the public to the private sector.

It was a revolutionary suggestion which, oddly enough, seems to have fallen flat. No other member of the government ventured to support or discuss it. The leaders of the other political parties remained discreetly silent. Even the news media were hushed. It was as if Mr. McKeough had made an unthinkable proposal, as if government sale of wine and spirits had been recognized throughout the world as the only possible method, and that any departure from it would be a sin against natural law and divine ordinance.

The reality, of course, is completely different. The provinces of Canada are the only governments in the western world which have adopted this impersonal and mechanical means of distributing one of man's most refined and sophisticated creations. Canada is so peculiar as to be unique, and it is interesting to speculate on why we have got so completely out of step with the rest of the civilized

---

Published in *The Globe and Mail*, headlined "Selling Liquor – A Bad Job the Government Way," on March 19, 1977.

world. Obviously government sale of wine and spirits must have some remote connection with the crusade for temperance or prohibition – the two words were often used interchangeably in Canada – during the nineteenth and early twentieth centuries.

Prohibition is an almost exclusively North American obsession. Both Canadians and Americans worked themselves into a most exalted state of moral fervour over the question, but they followed two quite different methods of dealing with it. In the United States, the comparative failure of the state prohibition laws led to a demand for federal legislation, backed by a constitutional amendment. In Canada, the federal law of 1878, the Canada Temperance Act, was attacked not because it failed to impose a real prohibition, but because it was alleged it invaded provincial rights.

Oliver Mowat, the Premier of Ontario, was a sanctimonious, self-righteous politician who once modestly referred to himself as a "Christian statesman," but who astutely kept clear of the dangerous issue of prohibition and never even attempted to deal with it by introducing a prohibition law. What interested him was not the promotion of temperance, but the revenue and political patronage which would certainly be realized through provincial regulation of the sale of beer, wine, and spirits. His Liquor Licencing Act of 1876 had converted every hotel owner or tavern keeper in Ontario into a red-hot Liberal, and the possibility that the Canada Temperance Act might change them back again into faithful Tories infuriated him.

He engaged Sir John A. Macdonald in a prolonged and angry battle over the conflicting claims of the federal power to enact laws for "the peace, order, and good government" of Canada, and the provincial right to impose "shop, saloon, tavern, auctioneer, and other licences." Before the nineteenth century ended, the British Judicial Committee of the Privy Council then and for long after the final court of appeal for Canadian constitutional cases, had decided in Mowat's favour, and the primacy of the provinces in the liquor trade had been solidly established.

It was the First World War that taught the provinces the vast possibilities of their new powers. The first decade of the twentieth century had brought a fervent revival of prohibitionist zeal, and in both Canada and the United States this was strengthened by the patriotic wartime impulse toward austerity and self-denial.

In the United States, Congress passed legislation forbidding the manufacture and sale of spirits, beer, and wine – an impressive example which by this time the Parliament of Canada was constitutionally incapable of following. It was left to the provinces to flex their newly developed legislative muscles, and during 1916 and 1917, all, with the exception of Quebec, enacted laws prohibiting the sale of liquor. Ontario characteristically exempted native wines from the general ban, and Quebec, which finally – and very briefly – joined the procession, exempted all wines as well as beer.

All this legislation was ostensibly enacted for the duration of the war, but in both Canada and the United States it had important, though sharply contrasting, post-war consequences. In the United States, it led directly to what was once called the "noble experiment," the eighteenth or Prohibition Amendment of the Constitution, and to thirteen appalling years of smuggling, bootlegging, adulteration, and gang warfare.

In Canada, the results were not nearly so drastic or spectacular: the chief consequence, in fact, was the growth of a characteristically cautious Canadian belief that although the continuation of total prohibition might be unwise, in the light of what was already happening in the United States, any return to the old pre-war state of free enterprise in the liquor trade would be still more deplorable.

As a result, the provincial governments of Canada were able, for reasons which now seem quite inexplicable, to persuade their gullible citizens that government sale of wines and spirits was an acceptable compromise between two highly undesirable alternatives. Modern Canadians, disillusioned with government in general and Crown corporations in particular, have learned to distrust the whole idea of the state in business; but during the 1920s the popularity of public ownership and control probably reached its climax in Canada. The Hydro-Electric Power Commission of Ontario – naïvely called the "People's Power" – had already proved the wisdom of public ownership. The newly created Canadian National Railways – the "People's Road" – would certainly confirm it.

During the twenties, all the provinces but Prince Edward Island established Crown corporations as the exclusive agencies for the sale of spirits and wine. Ontario was just as determined as the others to enjoy the large profits and useful patronage of government sales, but, on the other hand, it was equally determined not to offend the strong puritanical and prohibitionist sentiments of its citizens.

It managed to reconcile these two utterly opposed aims by what can only be described as a masterly exercise in doubletalk. It proceeded to act as if the open sale of liquor was a perfectly legitimate and proper activity of government, but that its consumption by the people of Ontario was depraved indulgence, which must be carried on inside private houses or hotel bedrooms.

It was not until 1934, the year after the eighteenth amendment had been repealed in the United States, that Premier Mitchell Hepburn finally legalized beer drinking in public, a liberty confined to drab, sparsely furnished taverns, quaintly called beer parlours, from which women were excluded and which quickly became as dirty and disreputable as the vanished saloons and bar rooms had ever been.

It was George Drew who ended this tyrannical and disgusting state of affairs. He acted in the belief that drinking wine and spirits was an agreeable social diversion and not a furtive private vice, and that it ought to take place in polite and civilized surroundings. In 1948, shortly before the provincial general election of June, his government legalized cocktail bars. The Tories lost seats in the election and Drew was defeated in his own constituency. He may have underestimated the surviving strength of prohibitionist feeling in the province, but the vote, which brought the Conservatives back to power with a still healthy majority over all parties, proved that the prohibitionists were now only a minority.

Drew's enlightened legislation stood, and Ontario, after more than two decades of evasive delays and mean, degrading compromises, had finally produced a reasonable set of regulations governing the consumption of wine and spirits.

The next duty of the Liquor Control Board of Ontario, as a responsible merchant, ought to have been to present its customers with the widest and most diversified range of liquors possible. It might even have tried to lure its hundreds of thousands of whisky drinkers to more refined and less potent liquors. Obviously, it did nothing of the kind. Its only apparent effort at the promotion of particular brands was to give a price advantage to Ontario native wines and Canadian rye whisky.

This was only a very minor consideration, and the main purpose of the Liquor Control Board was simply to make money for the Government of Ontario, an aim in which it was eminently successful from the very start. For the benefit of the Ontario treasury, it placed huge markups on its wares, with the comfortable assurance that if its clients didn't wish to pay these stiff prices, they would have to do without.

It was the people of Ontario, without any encouragement or instruction from their Liquor Control Board, who first became interested in the fascinating arcana of European wines. Gradually they began to recover some of the discriminating knowledge they had possessed in Victorian and Edwardian times and which the prohibitionists had managed to erase. Their patronage of the board's niggardly supply of wines increased so steadily that in the end, the board was forced to enlarge and diversify its stocks. Now the unbroken and apparently endless rows of whisky, gin, rum, and vodka are interrupted by more than a few token bottles of wine, aperitifs, and liqueurs.

Undoubtedly, the system of government sale, as it exists today, has a few merits. Liquor Control Board prices, though very steep, are uniform throughout the province, and the board tries to guard quality and strength. These certainly are benefits, but they are outweighed by the system's two major defects. In the first place, it is a monopoly, which provides its clients with only a selection, from which a good many firms and brands are necessarily excluded, and which are, of course, unobtainable anywhere else in the province. In the second place, it is a government operation, staffed by public employees, and not a commercial enterprise served by experienced and knowledgeable clerks.

Like some modern Canadian department stores, the Liquor Control Board shops are now simply oriental bazaars, with all the goods laid out on shelves, or racks, or tables, and the customer is left to make his own choice, without any assistance from the few remaining clerks, most of whom know little and care less about the stock in their charge.

Normally, the LCBO attendants are pleasant people, but they have certainly not been chosen for their expert and discriminating knowledge of wines and spirits. They are ignorant of the merits of rival brands and firms, and even of the qualities of different wine-producing regions. They have never heard of vintages. And, at the check-out counters they parcel up bottles as if they were bags of sugar or cartons of salt.

Prohibition is a dead issue, and the prohibitionists have vanished. But they have had their revenge – a curious revenge, which, of course, they never intended – on the peoples of Ontario.

Part Two

The Reviewers Reviewed

There can be no doubt that Canadian authors, as authors, often lead a precarious and anxious existence. There are undoubtedly more publishers in Canada than there were, and many more Canadian books are published than ever before; but this does not by any means imply that the average Canadian author can lead a life of affluence on the income from his book royalties. The word "royalty" has a fine, regal ring to it; but the author's royalty normally amounts to no more than 10 per cent of the retail price of the book, and the publisher and the bookseller divide the other 90 per cent between them. This meagre percentage might still bring in a fair return, if the Canadian public was a steady book-buying public. Unhappily it isn't.

In fact, the great majority of Canadians buy books only in the few short weeks before Christmas. If, at other times, they are moved by the strange, antisocial impulse to read a book, they don't buy it, they borrow it, usually from a public library. And, for this free use of his work, the Canadian author gets nothing at all. Public Lending Right, the system by which an author is paid in accordance with the popularity of his books with the patrons of public libraries, is already in operation in Australia and some of the Scandinavian countries. But it has not yet been established in Canada.

Published in *The Globe and Mail*, headlined "Literary Woes," on March 5, 1977.

Yet this is by no means the end of the Canadian author's woes. He has to live in a country which not only produces few steady book buyers, but which also tolerates a lot of very mediocre book reviewing. Book reviewing is, in fact, a foreign art which never became properly domiciled in Canada. The audience which might have welcomed it simply doesn't exist.

Normally, Canadians are interested in only a few classes of people – politicians, businessmen, trade unionists, scientists, economists, football players, hockey stars, and musical, theatrical, and television personalities. In comparison with these celebrated people, authors, particularly Canadian authors, hardly count at all; and the small esteem in which they are held is grotesquely evident in the treatment books receive in the daily press. Editorial writers, political commentators, economic analysts, sports writers, television critics, and so-called "columnists" – who often do no more than recount the essentially trivial events of their daily lives – monopolize the lion's share of the space left over from the news. Books are normally reserved for Saturday. And then they are lumped together with music, theatre, radio, and television, and labelled – in *The Globe and Mail* at least – as "Entertainment."

Books in Canada certainly suffer from inadequate space, infrequently given, for reviews; but they suffer still more from bad reviewers. This is partly because Canada does not possess, as England does, a group of what might be called "professional" reviewers – people who regularly review books for one or more journals, and who have built up a reputation as talented and knowledgeable critics. In Canada, there are very few professional reviewers; they are almost always amateurs, with little or no experience. Frequently, they do not even carry out a reviewer's first and basic duty – which is to tell the reader what the book is about and what were the author's evident intentions in writing it. Their unknown names arouse no interest and carry no authority; and all too often they attempt to compensate for their anonymity by painful attempts to be witty and hypercritical.

Canadian reviewers come, in the main, from three rather oddly assorted groups of people – journalists, and their friends and friends' friends, professors, and politicians. It's not surprising that

74

journalists should become book editors and reviewers, but it is rather more difficult to discover on what grounds they have been appointed. Is it perhaps because a veteran newspaperman, whose long and faithful service deserves reward, is put out to grass on the book page? Or has some young and eager journalist been given a promotion in return for his brilliant reporting of the town council or the magistrate's court? Or perhaps another young newspaperman has shyly confessed to writing a novel, and is at once appointed to the book page on the ground that he must, of course, know all about Canadian and English literature.

The second main source of Canadian book reviews is the professoriate of Canadian universities. In Canada, professors are quite frequently invited to review biographies, histories, literary studies, economic surveys, and political discussions. With some brilliant and conspicuous exceptions, they make, on the whole, a very mediocre job of it. Their chief defect is, of course, that they are very likely to be imprisoned by the narrow bounds of their academic specialty. The sad truth is that probably only a small minority are people of wide reading and general culture. They are indifferent to the literary quality, the arrangement, and the style of a book. Wit, irony, narrative skill, character drawing, descriptive or analytical power mean little or nothing to them.

They have spent long years grubbing in archives, libraries, and government departments to produce a thesis and win the coveted doctoral degree. This prolonged struggle has deepened, but has drastically narrowed, their interests. It has led them to place an exaggerated valuation on the evidence of unpublished documents – which they themselves have toiled so hard to get – and to depreciate seriously the merits of printed letters, diaries, memoirs and speeches. For these arid scholars, an incident or quotation taken, for example, from Pickersgill's *Mackenzie King Record*, or from Stacey's *A Very Double Life*, is inherently inferior to an incident or a quotation discovered in Mackenzie King's unpublished diaries, even though the printed passage may be much more pointed, characteristic, and revealing than the excerpt in manuscript.

Politicians – the third main group from which Canadian reviewers are chosen – is much smaller than the other two, though it is occasionally increased, particularly in Ottawa, by retired members of what we used to think of as the "civil service," though the American term "office holder" would probably be a good deal more appropriate now, when these Canadian office holders are all living such an affluent life on their big government salaries and indexed government pensions. Usually politicians are approached when the book editor decides that a confrontation between a Cabinet minister and one of his principal critics might be amusing. Thus, David Lewis was invited, by *Books in Canada,* to review a volume of John Diefenbaker's memoirs. A little while ago, Charles Taylor's trenchantly critical account of Canada's sorry performance on the International Control Commission in Vietnam, was given for review to Paul Martin, the former Secretary of State for External Affairs, and the minister mainly responsible for Canada's policy in the Far East.

These occasional literary intrusions by politicians and retired office holders, are, of course, only one manifestation of the dominance of politics over nearly every aspect of Canadian life. Canadian politics are still essentially party politics, despite the pompous rhetoric in which they are carried on; and simple old fashioned "partyism" still governs Canadian beliefs, attitudes, and even literary preferences in a fashion which would be quite impossible in an older country.

In England, an author who wrote a biography of Anthony Eden or Harold Wilson would not be instantly categorized as a red-hot socialist. Yet this is exactly what happens in Canada, occasionally with some show of reason, but usually with none at all. And once a political label has been affixed, it is never permitted to become unstuck even though an author may have expressly criticized or rejected the beliefs he is alleged to hold. The reviewer thus becomes a megalomaniac who assumes that he doesn't need to bother with the contents of the book itself, because he possesses an intimate knowledge of the private workings of the author's mind.

For much of the sad state of book reviewing in Canada, there is a simple, basic explanation. Unlike England or France, Canada has very little interest in, or respect for, literary values. The big

Canadian department stores provide ample evidence of this, for Canadians are, above everything else, consumers, buyers. Book departments have degenerated into collections of paperbacks, varied by expensive coffee-table books. Book cases, with a sliding glass door for each shelf, which used to be found in well-stocked furniture departments, have now totally disappeared. Their place has been taken over by radios, television sets, record players, and elaborate private bars. The *per capita* index of household libraries in Canada was probably never very great, and one suspects that in most houses built during the last quarter-century, books have virtually vanished. Public libraries have certainly increased in number, particularly in a wealthy province like Ontario; but the public library sale of a book in Canada could never cover the cost of production, as it was confidently assumed to do in England, at least until quite recently.

A feeling for literary values can be cultivated only through the study of languages and literatures. And this is precisely what a Canadian pupil or student is highly unlikely to get from his primary and secondary schools. He does not have to buy, he is lent, the textbooks he needs. He never gets into the habit of regarding a book as a valued personal possession, and he is impressed by the expensive audio-visual equipment in which his school has invested so lavishly. He sticks with languages as long as he has to; but, as he climbs higher on the educational ladder, he discovers that the new and fashionable educational philosophy – "do your own thing and have fun" – permits him to get rid of them. He drops Latin, one of the main sources of English. He will probably continue French, not because it has a noble literature, but because Canada has been officially proclaimed a bilingual country, and it has become politically meritorious to speak – though not necessarily to read or study – the French language. Once again politics has triumphed over literature.

After nearly a decade of this kind of schooling, the student reaches a university or a community college. He lacks the basic skills which are necessary for the use of his own mother tongue. He is virtually illiterate, or, at best, semi-literate. The university authorities have at length discovered this astounding truth, though it is difficult to understand why it took them so long to do so. They have imposed tests on their first-year students and prescribed remedial courses in English in the hope of correcting the appalling ignorance which the tests have revealed. They are, in fact, providing primary instruction in an institution supposedly devoted to higher learning. It is a preposterous contradiction, and the gap between a university's professed aims and the real accomplishments of its students grows steadily wider. Students who can barely write a tolerable English sentence are permitted to enrol in senior courses in Elizabethan Drama, the Modern Novel and Book Publishing.

Yet these are the people who will become the Canadian readers – and reviewers – of the future. Canadian authors are never likely to escape from their clutches.

"The Dictionary of Canadian Biography"

The *Dictionary of Canadian Biography* is one of the several major publication projects now being carried out in Canada. At Queen's University, a group of scholars are preparing an annotated edition of *The Collected Letters of Benjamin Disraeli*, the Tory statesman of mid-Victorian Britain. At Toronto, the University of Toronto Press has undertaken the publication of both an English translation of *The Collected Works of Erasmus*, the Dutch scholar, humanist, and theologian, and of *The Collected Letters of Emile Zola*, the French naturalistic novelist of the late nineteenth century. These certainly are large enterprises; but the scholarly work which they involve – the definition and annotation of existing texts – is essentially editorial in character. *The Dictionary of Canadian Biography* is a very different undertaking. It is an original work, composed of new articles on a broad selection of important historical Canadians, each written by a recognized authority on the subject.

The preparation of the *Dictionary* was made possible by a bequest of the late James Nicholson, a Toronto businessman, who left the bulk of his estate to the University of Toronto for the purpose of compiling and publishing a biographical reference work for Canada which could take its place alongside the British *Dictionary of National Biography*. Work began in 1959 under the first

---

Published in *The Globe and Mail* on February 19, 1977.

general editor, George W. Brown, a professor in the Department of History, University of Toronto; and it was Brown who made the basic decisions which determined the character of the *Dictionary*. He decided that, unlike the *Dictionary of National Biography*, which was arranged alphabetically throughout its sixty-five volumes, the *Dictionary of Canadian Biography* would be organized chronologically in periods, each period extending over a definite number of years, with an alphabetical arrangement of its contents. The first two volumes to be published covered the periods from 1000 to 1700 and from 1701 to 1740. Canadians of some distinction, who died within one of these two pairs of dates, formed the subject matter of the volumes.

In 1967, came another change in the development of the *Dictionary*. It was never intended that the volumes should necessarily follow each other in strict chronological sequence. Brown had hoped that research on the late nineteenth century could be begun before work on the eighteenth and early nineteenth centuries had been finished; and in 1967, the Centenary of Confederation, a large grant from the Centennial Commission enabled the second general editor, Professor David Hayne, and his associates to make a new beginning, starting at 1850. From then on, the work of the *Dictionary* has been carried on, with equal vigour, along two historical fronts, a volume on the late nineteenth century alternating with one on the late eighteenth. The third volume to be published, number X in the series, covered the decade 1871 to 1880. Volume III, which appeared two years later in 1970, dealt with the thirty years from 1741 to 1770.

The new volume, numbered IX, returns to the late nineteenth century and covers the decade 1861 to 1870. It is a bigger book than its nineteenth-century predecessor, Volume X, with a larger number of biographies, and its cast of characters is certainly varied and interesting. There are articles on such politicians as D'Arcy McGee, Louis Lafontaine, and William Lyon Mackenzie; on churchmen like Bishop John Strachan of Toronto and Bishop George Mountain of Quebec; on entrepreneurs such as Thomas Molson and William Dow, the brewers, and John Redpath, the sugar refiner; and on writers like T.C. Haliburton and F.-X.

80

Garneau. It is certainly a distinguished company, perhaps even more distinguished than that of Volume X, though Volume X contained the biographies of such towering political figures as George Brown, Sir George Cartier, and Louis-Joseph Papineau.

A half-century ago – even thirty years ago – it would have been simply impossible to produce the detailed information contained in Volume IX. The historians and antiquarians of the nineteenth and early twentieth centuries, led by Francis Parkman, had concentrated their interest on the French regime and the first formative decades of British rule. It was not until after the Second World War, when Canadian history had finally won an important place in the curricula of Canadian universities, that an increasingly large number of younger historians began serious research on the problems and personalities of Victorian Canada. Since then, the work has proceeded so fast and so far that it might be difficult now to discover an important character or an issue that has not become the subject of some book or doctoral thesis. An immense body of knowledge has been systematically built up; and the great merit of the *Dictionary of Canadian Biography* is that it appropriates this detailed information and distils it in concentrated form for the student and general reader.

The contributors to this and the other volumes of the *Dictionary* were all advised that "each biography should be an informative and stimulating treatment of its subject presented in a readable form." This was an invitation to escape from the formal portraits and frequently leaden style once thought appropriate for works of reference. On the whole, the contributors have successfully responded to it. They have dealt with the personalities – the qualities, defects and idiosyncrasies of their subjects – as well as with their beliefs, aims, and achievements. Inevitably, they have been obliged to make judgements; and while these judgements certainly increase the interest and vitality of the biographies, they are also extremely well-informed, based on detailed research and careful reflection. Bishop John Strachan and William Lyon Mackenzie are among the most controversial figures in Canadian history, but their biographies seem to me to be models of critical yet sympathetic evaluation. They are also well-organized and well-written. They are, in fact, highly readable short essays in the art of biography.

Volume IX, like the other volumes, is priced at $25. In the present inflated cost of books in Canada, this seems to me to be an undoubted bargain, and I frankly recommend all interested Canadians – general readers as well as students – to buy a copy. They will learn more about early Victorian Canada than they probably could from a dozen different biographies and histories.

Arnold Bennett's
Young Wives

Arnold Bennett died in March 1931, of typhoid fever, supposedly contracted in Paris. That was nearly fifty years ago; but the whole truth about certain aspects of his life, including his relations with women, has remained untold until now.

Yet two women, Marguerite Soulie and Dorothy Cheston, exercised a profound and highly unfortunate influence upon him and his career. Marguerite Soulie was a Frenchwoman whom Bennett married in middle life and from whom he subsequently secured a legal separation. Dorothy was a much younger Englishwoman, who became his mistress, bore his only child, and adopted the surname Bennett by deed poll, since Marguerite refused to grant her husband a divorce.

Both, in their very different ways, were demanding, assertive, and combative women; and both, unfortunately for the record, outlived Bennett by a great many years. Marguerite died in 1960; Dorothy, who attained the great age of eighty-six, lived on until nearly 1977.

By that time, most of Bennett's contemporaries, who could have revealed part or all of the truth about his domestic life, were dead and gone; but fortunately Frank Swinnerton, probably his closest friend, survived and now approaches the fabulous age of ninety-four. This book is the reward of his triumph and longevity. He has called it *Arnold Bennett: A Last Word*. On the subject of

Published in *The Globe and Mail*, headlined "The Truth About Arnold Bennett's Rocky Romances," on June 5, 1978.

Bennett's private life, it must indeed be regarded as *the* last word.

It is a relatively short book and makes no attempt to give a connected, chronological account of Bennett's life, or to provide a critical analysis of his work. Instead, Swinnerton concentrates on Bennett's character and personality, on his qualities of heart and mind, his beliefs and values, his habits and indulgences, his mannerisms and idiosyncrasies.

Swinnerton has always insisted that his friend was persistently misunderstood and misjudged by people who knew him little, if at all, and who all too frequently were jealous and resentful of his great popularity, prestige, and influence. This book is an attempt to restate and sum up all the evidence against these ignorant and malicious charges. Its other – and no doubt, its main – purpose is to tell frankly and without reserve the true story of the shipwreck of Bennett's marriage with Marguerite Soulie, and the ruin of his liaison with Dorothy Cheston.

By the 1920s, Bennett had become a very prominent author and an inviting target for jealous literary abuse. He was a popular novelist, a successful playwright, and a highly influential literary critic; his reviews in Beaverbrook's *Evening Standard* could make or break the fortunes of a book. His yacht, his well-cut clothes, his frequent supper parties in London's most expensive hotels, all seemed to prove that he was indeed the corpulent rich man of Max Beerbohm's cartoon. He looked invulnerable; but, in fact, he was fairly easily open to unfriendly attack.

The flat northern "a" of his native Staffordshire, which still lingered in his speech, as well as its harsh, explosive delivery, which was largely the result of his incurable stammer, could make him sound ill-bred and rude. Thus he could be ridiculed either as a coarse, uncultivated provincial, who had never outgrown his lowly origins, and was still dazzled by affluence and splendour; or he could be mocked as a literary emperor who was interested only in money and power and who used his position as a reviewer to enhance his own reputation. Ezra Pound, Wyndham Lewis, and two members of the Bloomsbury group, Clive Bell and Virginia Woolf, all took part in this critical game.

The ire of Virginia Woolf, whom Swinnerton describes as the

"High Priestess of the Bloomsbury sect," had been roused by a brief review which Bennett wrote of one of her early books.

It was one of Bennett's principal literary beliefs that the greatness of a novelist lay in his ability to create memorable characters, and he complained that the characters in *Jacob's Room* did not "vitally survive" in the mind. Virginia Woolf, who was and remained hypersensitive to the slightest and most casual criticism of her work, was furious. She wrote a reply, which appeared first in T.S. Eliot's *Criterion* magazine, and was later published as a pamphlet with *Mr. Bennett and Mrs. Brown* as its title.

In this, she attacked Bennett's detailed, realistic method of creating his characters and describing their environment. How, she asked scathingly, could such a gross materialist hope, by piling up external details, to reach and reveal the soul of even a commonplace woman like Mrs. Brown? It was an aggressive attack, but it seems to have left Bennett almost, if not entirely, unmoved.

At T.S. Eliot's suggestion, he began, but never finished, a reply. He accepted criticism as freely as he gave it. For him, it was all a legitimate part of the literary life.

This generous instinct for tolerance and compromise is evident not only in these literary encounters, but also in the tragedies in his relations with both Marguerite Soulie and Dorothy Cheston.

Bennett married Marguerite in 1907. Slight signs of strain began to show themselves fairly early in their life together; and these increased during the First World War, when Bennett was busy with war work in Beaverbrook's Ministry of Information.

Marguerite liked attention, wanted people to make a fuss over her, and, when she couldn't get this continuous deference from a preoccupied Bennett, tried to find it in other people. Eventually she discovered a young Frenchman named Pierre le Gros, who became an admiring and solicitous friend, though not apparently a lover. She was devoted to him, bought him expensive presents, including clothes, and paid for their travels together.

She then went to Bennett and abruptly demanded that her already generous dress allowance be doubled. Bennett replied that this was impossible unless he sold his country house or his yacht.

Marguerite had already shown a readiness to give vent to furious displays of temper when what she considered her rights were refused, or when she felt herself slighted or ignored. She now angrily declared that if he refused her request, she would leave him. She may have been surprised when he temperately replied that, in that case, she had better consult a solicitor. The result was a legal separation in which Bennett granted her a very generous financial settlement.

It might have been expected that, after this ordeal, Bennett would keep women at a respectful distance; but only six months later, in 1922, he met Dorothy Cheston, an actress, and slipped rapidly into a second entanglement, which quickly became just as abrasive and costly as the first.

Marguerite had been dark and dramatic in her appearance; Dorothy was a dazzling blonde, very English in her looks, full of immense vitality, and obsessed with ambition for theatrical success. Bennett was attracted to her; and she, Swinnerton believes, attached herself to him because he was a successful playwright and an apparently rich man with important theatrical connections, who would be able to forward her career.

The birth of a child, Virginia, in 1925, made her hold upon him secure. At his suggestion, she added Bennett to her name and went openly to live with him. In what had been a very well-regulated establishment, she was a highly disruptive force.

She grew more imperious, demanding, and quarrelsome. She wore Bennett out with endless theatrical gossip and all-night supper parties. She wasted his hard-earned money in repeated theatrical ventures which were either dubious successes or total failures. As the decade drew to a close, they passed from serious disagreements to open quarrels.

By 1930, when he was sixty-three, and a chronic victim of neuralgia and sleeplessness, Bennett had had enough. He proposed separation to Dorothy and Dorothy instantly demanded a financial settlement as lavish as Marguerite's. Their future was dark and unsettled when they left in December for a brief holiday in France. There Bennett contracted typhoid fever and the first symptoms of the dread disease began to appear in January, after their return to

London. Two months later, on the night of March 29, Bennett died.

Next morning, at Dorothy's urgent request, Swinnerton hurried over to the Bennett flat and, at her suggestion, entered the room where his old friend lay. For a moment they both stood gazing at his pallid face and shrunken form; and then Dorothy, catching sight of the translucent brandy-coloured ring that Bennett always wore on the little finger of his left hand, moved quickly across the room and wrenched it off.

"There was no suggestion," Swinnerton remarks, "that the ring was to be a treasured keepsake. She was appropriating something she fancied."

Swinnerton was appalled; but he felt for her in her bereavement and was touched by her complaint that none of Bennett's old friends had tried to sympathize with her. She mentioned particularly H.G. Wells, who lived in a flat in the same apartment, a few floors above; and Swinnerton agreed to go up and ask Wells to pay her a brief visit. The day before, he had written an appreciation of Bennett for one of the London newspapers and he found Wells reading it with tears in his eyes. Swinnerton gave him Dorothy's message, and asked him to go down to condole with her.

"No, I won't!" Wells almost screamed. "She's a bitch; and she killed Arnold!"

There was, as Swinnerton observed, no more to be said.

"Somerset Maugham and His World"

A comprehensive biography of Somerset Maugham will never be written. The materials for such a thorough, documented study simply do not exist, and Maugham himself is chiefly responsible for their disappearance.

He systematically destroyed letters and manuscripts. He preferred to be remembered and judged by his published work; and fortunately for those who want to know something about the man as well as the author, his published works were not limited to his novels, plays, and short stories, numerous though they are. He also wrote several books, beginning with *The Summing Up* – which sounded like a last word, but definitely wasn't – about himself, his methods, his travels, and his views on a wide variety of matters. It is on these books, and on his prefaces and introductions to the work of others that the author of a critical study of Maugham's career must chiefly rely. He will get some help also from the recollections of Maugham's contemporaries, critics, and detractors. Even that violent, almost incoherent diatribe, Beverly Nichols' *A Case of Human Bondage*, offers some information. But there is far more enlightenment in *Somerset and All the Maughams*, Robin Maugham's anecdotal family history, with its affectionate but very candid reminiscences of Somerset.

Frederic Raphael, the author of *Somerset Maugham and His World*, has his own little memoir to add to the large heap built up

---

Published in *The Globe and Mail* on June 4, 1977.

88

by others. In 1954, when Maugham was eighty, and he "a young and unpublished writer," Raphael daringly wrote to the Old Party – as Maugham called himself in his introductions to his television dramas – received an invitation to tea, and found a courteous and interested host who, for a brief moment when a lighted match fell from his fingers, suddenly became an old man "in a little panic of elderly nervousness." "I felt a great pity and affection for him," Raphael remembered. This affection, though qualified by a critical examination of Maugham's work and character, informs the whole of Raphael's book. It is a balanced study; good biographies are never written by debunkers.

Somerset Maugham and His World is just as full of solid biographical information as Timothy O'Sullivan's biography of Thomas Hardy, and it is much better written than C.P. Snow's life of Trollope. Like both these books it is an illustrated biography. The pictures, which include a number of scenes from Maugham's plays and television dramas, provide a fairly good record of the Old Party in England and Europe, but they give us no glimpse of his wanderings with Gerald Haxton in the Far East, upon which so much of his fiction was based. It's a pity Haxton didn't take a camera with him.

Raphael's crisp, pointed, frequently witty style is admirably adapted to his dispassionate review of Maugham's work and character. He makes no attempt to hide the spiteful malevolence which seems to have been a part of Maugham's nature from the beginning, and which grew more savage as he grew older.

Looking Back, Maugham's last book of recollections, with its venomous attack on his dead wife, Syrie, Raphael regards as completely inexcusable. He laments this dreadful postscript to an unhappy marriage; but, on the other hand, points out that it was an ambiguous relationship from the beginning. It started as a liaison between Maugham and Syrie Wellcome, the beautiful and fashionable wife of the elderly Henry Wellcome, who was supposedly a very complaisant husband, but who, after years of passive acquiescence, suddenly began divorce proceedings. The public opinion of the time required an honourable man to marry the woman in whose divorce he was cited as a correspondent, and

Syrie apparently supported this code of proper conduct with her own vehement entreaties. Maugham began married life with the resentful feeling that he had been trapped.

Raphael's appreciation of Maugham's work is just as detached and acute as his assessment of Maugham's character. He quotes, at some length, Edmund Wilson's notorious denunciation of the short stories as "magazine commodities . . . on about the same level as Sherlock Holmes"; but he also reminds the reader that as a writer Wilson had signally failed in all the departments in which Maugham had incontestably triumphed. Maugham's great wealth, his world-wide popularity, and his apparent invulnerability to criticism, made him an inviting target for envy and malice; but this, as Raphael observes, does not entirely account for the fact that despite *Of Human Bondage*, *The Moon and Sixpence*, and *Cakes and Ale*, "He never obtained critical favor at the highest level." Maugham turned out stories like "The Painted Veil" – "a piece of professionalism with no claim to originality or profundity" – far too easily and often for his own reputation. He was a splendid storyteller, with a highly observant, sceptical eye, and a fund of worldly wisdom, who was never inspired by anything in earth or heaven. "He is not a great writer," Raphael concludes, "and yet he is on the side of greatness."

"The Master Mariner"

This is a very unusual novel. It is, so the blurb on the jacket informs us, the realization of Nicholas Monsarrat's most ambitious dream as a writer. For twenty-five years he has lived with the vision of a vast, panoramic novel that would survey, through the eyes of a single protagonist, four centuries of British maritime history. Obviously, his protagonist could not be an ordinary mortal man. Of necessity, he could only be a fabulous being, perennial if not exactly eternal, who could reach the end of four hundred years of existence and emerge still endowed with the physical and mental equipment of his young manhood. Matthew Lawe became such a mythical creature, but only after his appalling act of cowardice and the curse that was its punishment had completely altered his nature. When his story opens, he is an ordinary young seaman, about twenty-two years old, who came from Barnstaple in Devon and happened to be a devoted follower of Sir Francis Drake.

The coming of the great Spanish Armada in 1588 was the prelude to Matthew Lawe's transmutation. He took part in the running fight up the English Channel and helped to force the Spanish ships to take refuge in the harbour of Calais. To smoke them out, Vice-Admiral Drake decided to use a familiar device of naval warfare at the time – the dispatch of fire-ships, small vessels

Published in slightly shortened form in *The Globe and Mail*, October 7, 1978.

set on course and fired at the last minute – against the huddle of Spanish ships in Calais roadstead. Matthew Lawe was chosen to command one of the fire-ships; but at the crucial moment, his paralyzing sense of fear, which had been mounting steadily during the engagement, took complete possession of him. He fired his ship too early, alerted the Spaniards, and partly spoilt Drake's plan. To save himself from capture, and from his own shame, he dived into the water and swam to shore, only to be caught by the enemy in the end.

Weeks later, after the dwindling armada had fled northward and around the Orkney Islands, one of its ships – the ship in which Matthew Lawe was imprisoned – took refuge in the harbour of Tobermory on the Isle of Mull. There the Spaniards captured "a wild, half-human, half-ape of a woman," a witch called Morag, who claimed the power of prophecy; and Matthew was haled from his prison in the hold to translate her incomprehensible Scottish speech. Urged by her captors to show her prophetic gifts, she predicted the total destruction of the Spanish ship in Tobermory harbour. The infuriated Spaniards threatened death to both the hag and her interpreter; but Morag, now at the extremity of her own life, declared that Matthew Lawe was untouchable. "He is beyond your power," she asserted. "We tell you you cannot kill this man. He will not die . . . . He will wander the wild waters . . . until all the seas run dry."

This was the curse – or the blessing – that henceforth governed Matthew Lawe's existence; and *The Master Mariner: Book 1, Running Proud* is the first instalment of his enormous saga. It begins in July 1588, with Lawe as the coxswain of Vice-Admiral Drake's flagship and ends in October 1805, with Captain Matthew Lawe as a witness of the death of Admiral Nelson off Cape Trafalgar. These were perhaps the two points of highest naval eminence in a life that was varied, but harsh and hazardous throughout. With Henry Hudson, Lawe sought a northwest passage to China and found only the land-locked frustration of Hudson Bay. He joined the crew of the fabulous buccaneer, Henry Morgan, and knew all the excitements and horrors of seventeenth-century piracy in the Caribbean and along the Spanish Main. A quiet, pleasant interval followed, in which he served as a clerk in the navy office presided over by Samuel Pepys, but all his money was lost in the South Sea Bubble, he was imprisoned for debt, and purchased his freedom only by accepting virtual slavery as a fisherman on the Grand Banks off Newfoundland. Captain James Cook, on his way westward to Quebec, freed him from this servitude; and with Cook, Lawe sailed up the St. Lawrence, and witnessed the siege of Quebec and the Battle of the Plains of Abraham. "I plan to survey the world," Cook had declared, and Matthew Lawe followed him in the *Resolution* on the voyage that ended in Cook's murder on the shores of the island of Hawaii. That was in 1779; and it was in 1793, fourteen years later, when Britain had declared war on the new French Republic, that Lawe joined Nelson's squadron in the Mediterranean, and in 1805, twelve years further on, he saw the fatal bullet strike his Admiral on the deck of H.M.S. *Victory*.

In October 1928, almost exactly half a century ago, Virginia Woolf published *Orlando*, the story of a being who lived, "with a change about from one sex to the other," from 1500 until modern times. In its time scheme, *Orlando* slightly resembles *The Master Mariner*, but otherwise no two books could be more conspicuously different. *Orlando*, perhaps the most popular work of a difficult and sometimes obscure writer, was an easy, amusing, light-hearted narrative. *The Master Mariner* is, on the whole, a harsh and sombre saga. Its characters indulge at times in coarse humour and sardonic wit: but in the main, its seven sections, each of which is well-illustrated with a map, are simply different variations on the main themes of privation, brutality, danger, cruelty, and death. These fearful challenges evoke the virtues of courage, endurance, and resolution, the very virtues that have made the glory of the British naval tradition. It is this "rough island story" that has fired the imagination of Nicholas Monsarrat, and he has brought to its telling all the trenchancy and vitality of his style. *The Master Mariner* is a harsh, gripping saga, not intended for the squeamish or the tender-minded.

My Father
and the United Church

In 1894, when my father, W. B. Creighton, graduated with honours in theology from Victoria College, there is no doubt that he expected to follow what was then the usual career of a minister of the Methodist Church of Canada. He was stationed first at Tupperville, a village deep in southwestern Ontario. After four years, which was the usual term of a pastoral charge in those days, he was transferred to another, still smaller southwestern Ontario hamlet called Giles, whose name has subsequently disappeared, at least from the official road maps of the province. It was at Giles that a serious physical weakness, a kind of laryngitis, first appeared, and began to threaten his career as a preacher. For about six months, while his wife and elder son, John Harvie, found a refuge in the farm of the senior Creightons, at Dorchester, Ontario, my father sought a cure in the milder climate of British Columbia. He was much better when he came back, but he was by no means cured of his fundamental weakness; and to the end of his life, he found difficulty in speaking in public before a large congregation. Obviously he had to find other work; and probably through the influence of his mother-in-law, Mrs. Eliza Jane Harvie, who was then a prominent figure in the early welfare services of Ontario, he was engaged in 1901 as the assistant editor of the *Christian Guardian*.

Five years later, in a race against two other Methodist clergymen, he was elected editor by the General Conference. This victory must have been greeted with jubilation by the Creighton household at 262 Concord Avenue, Toronto; but as a small boy of about four years old, I could have had no very clear idea of what the rejoicing was about. I remember, however, that somewhat later I was shown a postcard, with three match-stick figures running hard, and my father in the lead. I suspect that my father, as a mere assistant editor, had not been appointed to attend the conference, and that the postcard had been sent by an official delegate who had been present to witness his friend's triumph. I seem to remember that the postcard was carefully preserved for some time; but unfortunately it did not become a permanent document in the Creighton family archives.

It was not until years later, when the First World War began and I grew to be a teenager, that I began to appreciate the character and quality of the *Christian Guardian* under my father's editorship. What delighted me then, and what has never ceased to impress me since, were the range and catholicity of the paper's interests. If it had been simply a weekly record of Methodist happenings in Canada, it would have had little appeal to me; but from the days of its first editor, Egerton Ryerson, the paper had never been confined within these narrow limits, and my father tried constantly to extend and diversify its coverage of political issues, economic and social questions, and literary events. He enlisted the help of several correspondents in the United Kingdom, and subscribed to a number of British and foreign periodicals, including the weekly edition of the London *Times*. What was even more important, from my point of view, was his attempt to review new books, as they were published, and without any narrow emphasis on denominational or devotional literature. Not infrequently, he asked specially qualified people to review particular works; but the pressure of producing a weekly periodical with an editorial staff of three, made detailed correspondence with reviewers virtually impossible, and very often my father reviewed, or briefly noticed, the new books himself.

There was no time for reviewing in his office in the old Wesley Buildings on Richmond Street, or in the new Methodist Book and Publishing House on Queen Street West. Most of what my father wrote for the *Christian Guardian* or the *New Outlook* was written at home, in the evenings, after dinner. In his book-lined study, he composed a great many of the short "sermonettes," which used to appear on the cover of the *Guardian*; and there also he did his book reviewing. At certain seasons of the year, particularly in the early spring or in the last few weeks before Christmas, he would bring home several large parcels of books. A car would have made it easy to transport these parcels from the office to the house; but my father never had enough money to buy a car, and the books had to be carried by hand, in crowded streetcars, with at least one transfer, all the way from downtown Toronto to the west end. At home, the parcels were placed in the lower hall of our house, and I was given the delightful privilege of opening them, and looking over, and sampling, the books inside. It was a very rare occasion, I seem to remember, when I did not discover at least two or three volumes that interested me.

Keeping up with the new books was, my father considered, one of the important minor functions of every weekly periodical; but the chief obligation of a church weekly such as the *Christian Guardian* or the *New Outlook* was something quite different and much larger. Its main purpose, he thought, was to analyze and discuss, with Christian values always in mind, the chief religious, social, and political problems of the day. For this task he was singularly well-fitted, for his greatest gift lay in his writing ability. He was not particularly effective in debate. Long arguments in committee bored him; and his dislike of post-mortem discussions was so great that on one occasion, when a ring at the telephone threatened a renewal of some tiresome argument in committee, he stepped outside the back door of our house and asked my mother to inform the caller that he was "out." He was not a debater any more than he was a preacher; but he loved to express his thoughts in writing, and he wrote with force and persuasive power, and in a simple, straightforward, unadorned style that carried conviction to the great mass of his readers.

He was interested in a good many issues. In some he felt very strongly, and wrote with great vigour and simple eloquence. I was too young or too occupied with my own concerns to pay much attention to the various good causes which he undertook to support, but two at least stand out fairly clearly in memory. The most important of these was the First World War – the first great conflict in which Canada had engaged its full strength. My father hated the physical facts of war – its purposeless destruction and its appalling loss of life – but he believed that the great moral purpose of the First World War would redeem its crimes. Like a great many thoughtful people, including a large number of clergymen, he saw it as the beginning of a new and peaceful age in international relations and a novel and wonderful era in human equality and social welfare.

As everybody knows now, and as my father realized fairly quickly after the peace, these expectations proved false; but the hope of a better post-war world dominated our household during those years. My brother, who was five years older than I, had been commissioned an officer in the 48th Highlanders. He was sent to France, was wounded, invalided home, and helped to train other young officers for service at the front. The war, for the Creightons, became a personal and family affair, and its world significance and political importance steadily increased. It was true that my father took a very disrespectful view of certain Methodist clergymen – including the General Superintendent, S.D. Chown – who paraded around in military uniform during the war, but on the whole we were a very patriotic family. My parents and my brother were strong supporters of conscription, Sir Robert Borden, and Union Government. I spent an exhausting summer as a teenage assistant on a market-garden farm east of Toronto.

The post-war disillusionment was almost as extreme as the wartime idealism had been. The hope of a peaceful world order was wrecked by the renewal of international dissension and by the League of Nations' failure to gain universal acceptance. This betrayal of all his hopes was too much for my father. In one of the cover editorials of the *Guardian*, he announced his belief in an apparently unqualified pacifism. The belief that war itself could be a great cleansing and reforming agency was totally rejected; but this rejection by no means implied that the hope of a better and more equitable society was abandoned. In fact, the war extended and strengthened, if it did not initiate, the campaign for social justice waged by the Protestant clergymen of Canada. Until the war broke out, their struggle had been waged chiefly for particular aims, like the prohibition of beer, wine, and spirits; but in 1918, the final year of the war, this limited reform programme was drastically extended. My father, along with Salem Bland, Ernest Thomas, T. Albert Moore and others, played a prominent part in this movement. He was one of the group that drafted the radical social and economic resolution which was adopted by the Methodist General Conference in 1918. He gave generous space in the *Guardian* to articles by advocates of what came to be called the "Social Gospel" movement. In the Winnipeg General Strike of 1919, his sympathies were definitely on the side of the strikers.

Two years later, when a printers' strike broke out in the Methodist Book and Publishing House, he seemed almost to reverse his previous stand. At the start, he took the side of the Book Steward, S.W. Fallis, against the striking printers. Later, he was alienated by Fallis's intransigence, and apparently joined Ernest Thomas in the search for a peaceful solution. For him, it was not a clear-cut, indisputable case, one way or the other. He knew that the Publishing House operated on a very narrow margin of profit; and he was convinced by the Book Steward's argument that church publishing was a virtually sacrosanct operation, which must not be threatened by such mundane affairs as labour disputes. It was a very embarrassing episode for Methodists with a social conscience. As the printers' strike ground on and on, some of the enthusiasm and conviction seeped out of the Social Gospellers' struggle to liberalize and humanize the new industrial Canada. In part, this vitality was diverted to new controversies and causes – the debate over pacifism, the movement for church union, and the vain attempt to save prohibition.

In part also, Canadian Protestants were giving up secular concerns entirely for new forms of evangelism; and one of the most fashionable of these was called Buchmanism or the "Oxford Group" movement. My father had never been impressed by the revivalist traditions of the old Methodist Church; and in the autumn of 1932, when the apostles of the Oxford Group arrived in force in Toronto, he was determined to investigate before he applauded. The Buchmanites preferred to carry on their mission in private houses, often the houses of the very rich, where they indulged in intimate personal confessions, known as "sharings," and not infrequently spiced with avowals of sexual guilt. My father attended some of these "house-parties" and was offended by what he regarded as their unpleasant mixture of wealth, self-complacency, and exhibitionism. He openly criticized the new movement in the editorial pages of the *New Outlook*, only to be confronted, in his turn, by the three senior clergymen of the United Church of Toronto, the Reverends George C. Pidgeon, Trevor H. Davies, and John R.P. Sclater.

In a public statement, printed in the *Globe* and the *Mail and Empire*, the three clergymen declared that my father's opinion of the Oxford Group "does not express the view of the United Church as a whole." Criticism of his editorial position was familiar enough to my father; but usually his critics spoke for themselves only and he was a little surprised that the three clergymen felt themselves entitled to represent the whole church. What grieved him most, however, was the fact that Pidgeon, Davies, and Sclater had not sent their protest to the *New Outlook*, where his editorial had appeared, but had preferred to have it printed in the morning newspapers of Toronto. They had, in fact, used the media to cover my father with an undeserved notoriety; and, to the best of my knowledge, not one of the three ever afterwards offered an explanation or an apology for what he had done.

It was a painful episode in my father's life. Denounced by the leading Toronto representatives of the United Church, he was also largely ostracized by the parishioners of Howard Park Church, which he had attended for over twenty years. In 1936, he finally retired from the editorship of the *New Outlook*, and a year later left the west end to live in central Toronto. On Sundays he often went to Yorkminster Baptist Church at the corner of Yonge and Heath Streets; and, so far as I know, he never again became a regular attendant at a United church.

Part Three

John A. Macdonald,
Robert Baldwin,
and the University of Toronto

The twenty-five years which separate the grant of the King's College Charter in 1827 from the opening of Trinity College in 1852, form one of the most extraordinary periods in the history of Canada. With the possible exception of the years of the British Conquest this quarter-century is probably more familiar to the average Canadian than any other in Canadian history. If the average Canadian knows of only one political figure, it is more likely to be William Lyon Mackenzie; and if he remembers any one political achievement, it is almost certain to be Responsible Government. The strength of these collective memories is obvious, yet curiously difficult to explain. Canadians on the whole have shown extremely little interest in history in general, and still less in their own. The events of this quarter-century are scarcely heroic or thrilling, and its principal characters can hardly be called creative or courageous. The interest of the period, in fact, is not really intrinsic at all. It lies not in the incidents and personalities themselves, but in the way they have been presented and interpreted. The truth is that the history of these twenty-five years, as it has been popularly presented for generations, is not mainly history at all. It is mythology.

Mythology, the dictionaries assure us, is a collection of traditional stories, dealing with such supernatural beings as heroes or

A lecture entitled "The Historical Setting of the Founding of the University of Toronto," given in the Larkin-Stuart sesquicentennial series at Trinity College, in the University of Toronto, on October 26, 1977.

heroic ancestors, and embodying some popular idea of historical phenomena. This, on the whole, is not a bad description of the popular notion of what happened in Upper Canada and Canada West from 1827 to 1852. If a good many scholarly studies had been written about the period, this semi-literate conception of its character and meaning might have been greatly altered; but the curious fact is that not a great many professional historians have been attracted to it. The school books go on talking in scandalized tones about the iniquities of the Family Compact, but no systematic study of its membership and operations has ever been made. Until recently, there were no biographies of that proud, scheming prelate, Bishop Strachan; and the latest biographical study of Mackenzie, published more than twenty years ago, was never intended to be a full-scale life. Even the Rebellion of 1837 itself, that heroic encounter which saved our liberties and gave us Responsible Government, has not been critically re-examined in modern times.

As a result of this strange lack of critical revision, the mythology of Upper Canada has remained largely untouched. It is varied only in accordance with what are thought to be the different intellectual capacities of that very small group, the readers of Canadian history. At the lowest level, the level of school books and popular accounts, the myth becomes an epochal struggle between the forces of light and progress and the powers of darkness and repression. On the one hand are courageous and dedicated democrats like William Lyon Mackenzie, wise, calm moderates like Robert Baldwin and Louis Lafontaine, and enlightened and beneficent governors like Sir Charles Bagot and Lord Elgin. On the other side are bigoted, overbearing churchmen like Bishop Strachan, bullying office-holders like J.H. Boulton and Christopher Hagerman, and obscurantist and dictatorial governors like Sir Francis Bond Head and Sir Charles Metcalfe. Even at a supposedly higher level of intelligence, these glaring contrasts do not entirely disappear; they simply take on the more imposing disguise of a conflict of principles or a class struggle. Whig historians see it as a momentous conflict between imperial governance and Responsible Government. Left-wing writers interpret it as a struggle between an aroused proletariat and an unbending autocracy. The form and decorations of the old myths are constantly changing, according to fashion; but their moral remains unaltered. Reform and progress are always right and always win; Toryism and reaction are always wrong and always lose. In that spirited little history of England, by Sellers and Yeatman, *1066 And All That*, the Royalists in the English Civil War are described as "wrong but romantic" and the Puritans as "right but repulsive." These generalizations could never be applied to the great era of rebellion and reform in Upper Canada. There the Reformers were both right and romantic, and the Tories both wrong and repulsive. In Canada, the good and the beautiful must always win.

II

Once these abstract, doctrinaire approaches to the history of Upper Canada are abandoned, the search for the origins of the University of Toronto become a human, complex, and interesting task. Our ancestors, the Canadians who lived through these twenty-five crowded years, inhabited a simple, inland, frontier province, but they cannot be viewed in isolation. They were very much dependent upon the outside world, and deeply influenced by it, and the age in which they lived was extremely turbulent. In almost every department of human thought and activity in western-European-American society, there were radical and painful changes. Politically it was the age of the Reform Bill in Great Britain, Jacksonian Democracy in the United States, and the Revolutions of 1848 in Europe. In the realm of faith and ecclesiastical order, it was deeply marked by the disruption of the Church of Scotland and the Oxford Movement in England. The abandonment of the Old Colonial System and the British adoption of free trade led to depression and disaffection in the colonies, particularly in British North America.

Education, particularly higher education, was subject to much the same vigorous reforming influences. Prominent public figures and learned periodicals began to demand drastic changes in the government, curriculum and teaching methods of the universities, as well as in their requirements for admission or for degrees. Oxford and Cambridge were sharply criticized for their exclusive concentration on the classics and mathematics and for their ignorant neglect of modern European studies in what were supposed to be their specialties. The Scottish universities had become renowned for their eighteenth- and early nineteenth-century figures, David Hume, Adam Smith, and Dugald Stewart, and for their work in logic and moral philosophy, history and political economy, physics and chemistry.

During the first half of the nineteenth century, the public debate over the rival merits of the two systems often became acute. The collegiate organization – a number of separate, residential colleges grouped together in a university – was frequently and very unfavourably compared with a university organized, as in Scotland, as a great single institution. The Scottish universities, it was proudly claimed, were open to all classes and all sects, while Oxford and Cambridge had become the private and exclusive preserve, carefully guarded by religious tests, for Church of England clergymen and members of the English governing class. Scottish critics ridiculed the plight of the Oxford and Cambridge undergraduate, who never came in contact with the great minds of his age, and had to be content with an incompetent college tutor, who was utterly unknown outside the walls of his own senior common room. Oxford and Cambridge apologists fought back by deploring the miserable existence of the Scottish students, who lived alone in sordid lodgings, never enjoyed any close contact with their professors, and gained their knowledge only through great public lectures which were often no more than theatrical displays.

The news of these educational controversies reached Upper Canada slowly, imperfectly, and at second hand. With one very important exception, none of the people who played an important part in the founding of the University of Toronto was a university graduate. Of the governors of the period, only Bagot and Elgin were Oxford men. Robert Baldwin, William Henry Draper, and John Alexander Macdonald, the three provincial politicians who sponsored the university bills of the 1840s, were all products of the Upper Canadian District Grammar Schools. The one conspicuous and significant exception to this nearly total lack of university experience was John Strachan himself, Bishop of Toronto. He gained his Master of Arts degree – the equivalent of Bachelor of Arts in other universities – at King's College Aberdeen; and his only senior degree was an honorary Doctorate of Divinity, also from Aberdeen. His entire university experience, his knowledge of university organization, curriculum, and teaching methods were exclusively Scottish; and it was as a school teacher in the Scottish tradition, first at Kingston and then at Cornwall, that he began life in Upper Canada.

The other great influence in Strachan's career as an educator was, of course, his Christian faith and his devotion to the Church of England. His parents had been nominally Presbyterian; but neither his father nor mother could be counted as a very devout member of the Church of Scotland or a very regular attendant at its services. When their son John came out to Canada in 1799, he was at least formally a Presbyterian; but five years later, shortly after he had made an unsuccessful private inquiry concerning a vacancy at the St. Gabriel Presbyterian Church in Montreal, he was ordained a priest of the Church of England in Canada. He did not, of course, suspect the truth, but this indiscreet private inquiry was carefully retained for a quarter-century by the supposed friend to whom it had been sent in confidence; and then, just at the significant moment of Strachan's appointment as Archdeacon of York, it was made public. His enemies seized on this dramatic revelation as a proof that Strachan had changed one communion for another in order to advance his career; and ever since, this episode has occasionally been regarded as a slight reflection on Strachan's sincerity. Oddly enough, no such discredit had ever been imputed to Egerton Ryerson and his brothers, who changed from Anglicanism to Methodism despite the vehement objections of their devout Anglican father. Evidently conversion from Anglicanism to Methodism has been generally accepted as praiseworthy by Canadian historians, while conversion from Presbyterianism to Anglicanism has been regarded as slightly questionable.

The strong religious convictions of the Canadians who lived

through this crowded quarter-century often broke out in acrimonious sectarian disputes; but these controversies never involved any basic disagreement about the centrality of religion in every aspect of human life. The emergence of the University of Toronto as a secular institution in the early 1850s did not imply any weakening of the belief in the indissoluble union of religion and education; it meant simply that the different churches were unable to agree on an acceptable common form of religious instruction and practice. The Methodists, Presbyterians, and smaller sects objected to King's College, because its original charter, secured by Strachan in 1827, gave its government and teaching into the control of Anglicans. Yet when these same Methodists and Presbyterians came to found colleges of their own – Queen's College at Kingston, and Upper Canada Academy, which soon became Victoria College, at Cobourg – they were just as firmly and exclusively under Methodist or Presbyterian control and direction as King's had ever been under Anglican.

Throughout the nineteenth century and well into the twentieth, every Principal of Queen's University was a Presbyterian clergyman and every President of Victoria College was a Methodist parson. Each institution quickly developed and tenaciously retained its characteristic and distinctive denominational ambience. Queen's exhaled an air of rather bleak Scottish austerity, Victoria an atmosphere of earnest, evangelical restraint. More than half a century ago, when I was a student at Victoria, I found that this ambience still persisted. At Victoria there were student promenades, but never student dances. There was a chapel where we sang robust Methodist hymns. And at least once a year a great campaign was launched on behalf of the Methodist missions in China. We were informed, in compelling tones, that in the Chinese provinces of Chu-bu or Bang-quang, or names to that effect, there were only two missionaries where at least fifty were urgently needed. In my final year at Victoria, when I was editor of *Acta Victoriana*, the undergraduate journal, I wrote an editorial criticizing these annual missionary drives. And I soon became aware of the displeasure of the authorities.

III

There are probably more myths about the politics of Canada during the quarter-century from 1827 to 1852 than there are about its religions or its education. Though the character of these myths varies considerably, most have a common basis in a distinctly erroneous conception of the nature of political life in Upper Canada. All too frequently it has been assumed that the controversy which reached its climax in the Rebellion of 1837 was a simple, almost classic case of a permanent Reform majority in the elected assembly confronting an appointed and irresponsible group of reactionary oligarchs immovably established in the Legislative and Executive Councils. It is true that the membership of these two senior bodies of government remained fairly stationary, although on one occasion an attempt was made to give the Reformers representation in the Executive. But it is also true that ever since organized political groups first began to make their appearance, the composition of the House of Assembly changed frequently and radically. In the nine years from 1828 to 1837, the year of the rebellion, there were four general elections in Upper Canada. The Reformers won two and controlled the Assembly for four years. The Conservatives or Constitutionalists, as they preferred to call themselves, won two and controlled it for five.

The myth about the character and fortunes of the party struggle in Upper Canada does not stand alone. There is another, perhaps even more important legend about its origins and rival political principles. The source of the conflict is generally assumed to lie in the perennial antagonism of those who want stability and those who want change. This simple conception of a clash between temperamental Liberals and instinctive Conservatives neglects the national feelings and loyalties which were some of the strongest political forces of the time. It is highly significant that the Reform Party began to take shape during the final stages of the long and acrimonious dispute over what was known as the Alien Question. In its essentials, the Alien Question concerned the right of the Americans in the province to vote, hold office, acquire property, and enjoy the other privileges of citizenship. The alarming significance of this question becomes clear when one remembers that down to about 1820, nearly everybody resident in Upper Canada was either an emigrant – or the child or grandchild of an emigrant – from what was about to become, or had become, the United States of America.

The true Loyalists of 1784 had been followed by the dubiously loyal "late Loyalists" and those in turn by other American immigrants, who continued to arrive until the War of 1812, and for some years after it was over, and whose main motive for settling in Upper Canada was simply a keen appetite for good, free land. The true Loyalists dominated the eastern division of the province; the later American settlers controlled the so-called Home District, with York as its capital, and the London and Western Districts beyond. In 1825, the Province of Upper Canada, particularly its western division, must have looked, and sounded, very much like one of the new midwestern American states, Ohio or Illinois. Americans, often newly immigrated, ran the hotels and taverns and taught in the schools. What would now be called "midwestern twang" must have been very audible around Toronto and through the west! In the eyes of the new British settlers and the members of the governing class in York, these new American immigrants were simply "Yankees" or "Republicans."

The coming of the great new wave of British immigration radically altered this situation. The movement began in the 1820s, continued, at intervals, for about thirty years, and reached its first peak early in the 1830s. Between 1830 and 1833, the population of Upper Canada increased by about 50 per cent. In general, the newcomers found homes for themselves in the regions north of the original American settlements. The great majority of them had left straitened circumstances in the Motherland and had come in the hope of economic and social betterment; but, in addition to these normal migrants, there were a significant number of people from an entirely different economic and social background. Substantial landowners, professional men with college educations, half-pay military and naval officers – people like the Moodies, Traills, Stricklands and Langtons – could rely on their pensions and some inherited capital, monies which enabled them to engage servants and to achieve a fairly comfortable style of life.

The coming of the British migrants fundamentally changed the whole political state of affairs in Upper Canada. The devotion to the imperial connection, to British institutions and British traditions of government, which the true Loyalists had brought with them, had been overlaid and almost extinguished by republican sentiments carried in from the United States. Now these old loyalties suddenly reappeared, stronger than they had been since the War of 1812, and just as militant as ever. The new British settlers joined with the true Loyalists in an instinctive political combination, and it is this union which provides the key to what happened in the 1830s. It is the real explanation of the victory of the Constitutionalists in the election of 1836, and the defeat of the Rebellion and the American invasions in 1837-38.

It is in these national loyalties that the political theory of the 1830s has its origin. It is the expression of the basic antipathy between two political inheritances and two political experiences, between monarchy and parliamentary government on the one hand, and republicanism and congressional institutions on the other. The Constitutionalists and the moderate Reformers under Baldwin both believed in the constitution of Upper Canada, as it was and as it would develop along British lines, though the Reformers were much more eager to hasten the process of development. It was Mackenzie and the rebels of 1837 who tried to convert the Upper Canadians to an alien allegiance: and the fact that Mackenzie is remembered today, not as a traitor, but as a beneficent reformer is perhaps the greatest of the political myths of the period!

His sculptured bust in Queen's Park, near the legislative building was placed there, so the inscription runs, "to commemorate the struggle for Responsible Government in Upper Canada." The simple truth is, of course, that Mackenzie never became, as Baldwin unquestionably did, the consistent advocate of Responsible Government as the sovereign cure for the political ills of Upper Canada. He mentioned it occasionally simply because, at one time or another, he mentioned practically all the fashionable political ideas and devices of the time. Mackenzie's mind was, in fact, an overstuffed rag-bag of other people's ideas; but there is no doubt that most of the scraps in this motley collection were borrowed from the United States. His Declaration of the

111

Toronto Reformers is full of echoes of Jefferson's Declaration of Independence; and his Draft Constitution for the State of Upper Canada is closely modelled, except for a few of Mackenzie's own idiosyncrasies, on the Constitution of the United States.

Mackenzie drew his military strength, such as it was, from the Home District in general and the County of York in particular, regions which had been settled mainly by Americans; and several of his principal followers, including Samuel Lount and Jesse Lloyd, had been born in the United States. Mackenzie fled to Buffalo, where he attempted to organize an American invasion of Upper Canada; and for nearly a year after the absurd little encounter on Yonge Street, American raids on the Canadian frontier continued, culminating in the Battle of the Windmill, near Prescott, in which more Canadian lives were apparently lost than in the Battle of Queenston Heights in 1812.

The flight of Mackenzie and the repulse of the American raids were swiftly followed by the mission of Lord Durham, the union of Upper and Lower Canada, and the triumph of Responsible Government. This is a period which has always been regarded with profound, almost reverential respect by Canadian historians; and to suggest that the sacred decade of the 1840s – the New Testament of Canadian history, it might appropriately be called – is largely a myth, or even that it contains mythical elements, is to risk the charge of historical heresy. The introduction of Responsible Government certainly meant the beginning of Cabinet rule and the development of recognizable political parties; but to assume that these new parties represented a real division between people of Liberal beliefs and Conservative convictions is a highly questionable assumption.

In the centre of every parliament of the Union, and of every parliament of the Confederation which followed it, there was, and is, a large, compact group of French-Canadian members whose fundamental aim is not to serve the fortunes of either party, but to protect and advance the interests of French Canada through any party that looks as if it has a good chance of getting and keeping political power. From 1841 to 1854, this was the Reform Party; from 1854 to 1896, it was the Liberal-Conservative Party of Sir

John Macdonald; and from 1896 on, it has been the Liberal Party of Laurier, Mackenzie King, St. Laurent, Pearson, and Trudeau. For such governments, the interests and demands of French Canada are always important; but when parties are evenly balanced or a minority government in power, the satisfaction of these demands becomes absolutely vital. Major concessions have simply got to be made in order to retain French-Canadian support. In our own day this has meant the establishment of the Bilingual and Bicultural Commission, the passage of the Official Languages Act, and the desperate efforts of Prime Minister Trudeau to entrench language rights in the Constitution of Canada. In the United Canada of the 1840s, it meant the removal of the legislature from Kingston to Montreal, the passage of the Rebellion Losses Bill, and the enactment of the Secret Societies Bill, which was directed against the Tory Orange Order, but did not touch the St. Jean Baptiste Societies, the new, strongly nationalist French-Canadian organizations which were founded in the 1840s.

IV

It was in these circumstances, intellectual, cultural, and political, that the University of Toronto had its protracted, difficult, and even agonizing birth. It began its existence with the famous, or notorious, Charter, which John Strachan, Archdeacon of York, secured from the British government in 1827; but for many years, about sixteen in all, it existed only on the parchment on which its terms had been inscribed. These terms were fairly generous for the time; they would have been still more generous if Strachan's own views had prevailed over those of the British government's other clerical advisers. Strachan certainly believed that the President of the University of King's College should be a Church of England clergyman; but he thought it invidious and unwise that a particular Anglican clergyman – himself, in fact, as Archdeacon of York – should be specified in the Charter. He had equally nothing to do with another of the Charter's highly controversial clauses, which required the professors and other members of the College Council to be members of the Church of England and to subscribe to the Thirty-Nine Articles. In fact, the only part of the Charter which truly reflects Strachan's liberal instincts in education is the clause which permitted students to enter King's College without meeting any religious tests. In an age when such tests completely excluded dissenters and Roman Catholics from all English universities, this was an astonishing innovation.

The fond hope that the Charter of the University of King's College would soon take on a visible and admirable form in the appointment of a learned group of professors and the construction of a handsome building was doomed to encounter apparently endless delays and postponements. The new Lieutenant-Governor, Sir John Colborne, was convinced that a secondary school on the English model was more suitable than a university to a frontier province; and he appropriated part of the university's magnificent endowment of 225,000 acres of Crown Land in order to found Upper Canada College. The Reformers in the Assembly, furious at the appropriation of such a magnificent grant for the benefit of a single religious communion, repeatedly passed bills for the drastic alteration of the Charter, bills which were thrown out with equal regularity by the Legislative Council. It was not until 1837 – ten years after the Charter had been granted – that the Legislature finally agreed on an amending statute, which was almost as extreme as those the Reformers had proposed. It retained a general Christian test for professors and officers, but it opened all appointments to candidates of all denominations, and added a lay element in the shape of representatives from the legislature and the government to the college council. Everything at last seemed ready, and tenders were called for the construction of a building when it was most unfortunately discovered that the college accounts, kept by the Bursar Colonel Wells, were in a state of chaos, and that Wells, on his own responsibility, had withdrawn considerable sums as loans to worthy Anglicans, including Bishop Strachan himself.

It was not until the spring of 1842, that the new Governor-General, Sir Charles Bagot, laid the cornerstone of King's College, and not until June of the following year that its doors were finally opened to students. In the meantime, the quarrelling politicians of the United Province of Canada had taken it upon themselves to interfere – and to keep on interfering – in its destiny. In the six years from 1843 to 1849, the provincial legislature actually debated four separate bills amending the original Charter of King's. Very fortunately, it is quite unnecessary to examine these separate measures in any detail, for their differences centred on one particular point. Would the legislature insist on a purely secular institution, or would it admit the denominational colleges, Victoria, Queen's, and Regiopolis, the small Roman Catholic institution at Kingston, to share in the teaching as well as in the income from the university's huge endowment?

There was no doubt at all about the stand that Robert Baldwin, the hero of Responsible Government, would take. His university bill of 1843 provided the maximum of centralization and very nearly the maximum of secularization. It abolished all religious tests, reduced the four colleges to the level of divinity halls or theological institutions, granted each of them an extremely small annual income, and subjected them all to the authority of a University Board of Control, a large body composed entirely of such non-academics as the Mayor of Toronto, the Sitting Members for Toronto and the Yorks, the Treasurer of the Law Society, and twenty other local bigwigs, all equally ignorant of the meaning and purpose of a university. Bishop Strachan regarded the Baldwin Bill as a monstrous measure, at once impious and tyrannical. William Henry Draper, the urbane and persuasive leader of the moderate Conservatives, who was known as "Sweet William," attacked it eloquently and at length in the Assembly. Yet, within a year, it began to seem that Draper's great show of moral indignation was more than a little rhetorical.

The general election of 1844 brought the Conservatives back to power, and Draper became Attorney-General West, the leading position in the ministry. It was a badly divided ministry with moderates like Draper and John A. Macdonald on one side, and ultras like William Boulton and George and Henry Sherwood on the other. Any university bill, even if it had been drafted in heaven, would almost certainly have threatened the uneasy union between these two groups; but the university question was urgent and Draper decided that he must try to settle it. In order to pacify his right-wing followers, he restored the colleges to their central position as teaching institutions, freed them from external lay control, and increased their annual grants. These concessions were rather more than palliatives; but they could not disguise the glaring fact that Draper's bill, in very much the same way as Baldwin's, had centralized higher education in a single federal institution and had transferred to it the whole of the original endowment of King's College. For the High-Church Tories, this was an act of manifest spoliation and sacrilege. Led by William Boulton, who spoke so frequently and earnestly on university affairs that he was nicknamed "Defender of the Faith" or "University Bill," they forced Draper to withdraw his measure.

Two years went by. The fortunes of the moderate and ultra divisions of the Conservative Party swayed backwards and forwards, like contending armies, across the floor of the Executive Council Chamber. Henry Sherwood was virtually dismissed from office, and Draper finally retired altogether from politics. John A. Macdonald was persuaded to join the ministry as Receiver-General but Sherwood returned in triumph as its Attorney-General. It was Macdonald's appointment that led to the last Conservative attempt to settle the university question. The two bills which he introduced in July 1847, in sharp contrast with Baldwin's and Draper's complicated measures, were extremely simple and concise. The whole conception of a great provincial university, with affiliated colleges, was completely abandoned. Instead, the higher education of the youth of Canada West was to be entrusted to the denominational colleges, as they were or as they originally had been, for Strachan's Charter of 1827 was restored, with only minor amendments, to King's College. All that remained of the idea of a university was a University Endowment Board, which was empowered to divide the annual income from the endowment among the colleges, giving £3000 annually to King's, and £1500 to Victoria, Queen's and Regiopolis, with the balance for the District Grammar Schools.

Strachan had actually consented to a division of the endowment. The ultra Conservatives were naturally in favour of Macdonald's bill, and both Methodists and Presbyterians were apparently ready to give it support. If the ramshackle coalition of moderate and right-wing Tories had been only a little stronger, Macdonald's university settlement very probably would have become the law of the land. If it had, it would have anticipated, though the differences are obvious and significant, the University Federation which was actually achieved generations later in Ontario. Macdonald's plan, in fact, came much closer to the twentieth-century organization of the Faculty of Arts and Science at the University of Toronto than any of the other university projects of the 1840s. It is tempting to speculate on what would have happened if his bill had passed. But it is a futile speculation, for the Conservative government was steadily losing strength in the Assembly, for other reasons than its educational policy; and in the end, Macdonald's bill, like all its predecessors, was prudently withdrawn. Less than two years later, after the Reformers had won a conclusive victory at the polls, Baldwin settled the university question, as he thought, for ever. He created a completely secular and centralized university, with three Faculties, of Arts, Law, and Medicine, and no affiliated colleges; and to this single and exclusive body he transferred the whole of the original endowment of King's College.

In the sense that it brought to a close the long, rancorous fight over Strachan's Charter of 1827, Baldwin's act of 1849 may be said to have settled the university question: but the assumption that it established a general and amicable agreement about higher education in Canada West is still another of the many myths of this agitated quarter-century. Baldwin had explicitly denied what the great majority of the people of Canada West implicitly believed, that there was an intimate and essential connection between religion and education. This great majority simply refused to accept Baldwin's denial. So strong and general was the popular protest against his "godless" university that the embarrassed legislature was obliged to pass a feeble explanatory bill asserting that the University Act of 1849 implied no hostile intent to religion!

This rather pathetic disclaimer did not carry much conviction. For years, the great new university, and its dependency, University

College, travelled about in an unhappy, migratory fashion, from one unsuitable habitation to another, collecting few students in its erratic and humiliating wanderings. It was not until 1859, ten years after Baldwin's bill had become law, when its impressive new building was finally completed, that University College began at last to prosper. In the meantime, Victoria and Queen's, declining the university's invitation to join it in a federal union, pursued their separate and independent ways. They were soon joined by the University of Trinity College, for which Bishop Strachan had secured funds in England, and which, in 1852, opened its doors to students, including some who had left the "godless" university for the new Anglican College. These two strong and radically different strains – secular and denominational – in Canadian thought about higher education, which are embodied in these rival institutions, showed an extraordinary vitality and persistence. The four colleges, one dependent on the state, the others supported by different religious communions, survived undaunted for decades; and it was not until generations later that three of them consented to unite their distinct personalities in a federation. John Alexander Macdonald and Robert Baldwin are both founders of the University of Toronto.

The Ogdensburg Agreement and F.H. Underhill

The Canadian Institute of Public Affairs, which meets annually at Geneva Park on Lake Couchiching, in Ontario, has apparently lost some of the prestige, or the notoriety, which once attracted so many prominent people to its sessions. There may be several reasons for this seeming decline. The lack of interesting and provocative speakers, the rivalry of the television panels, interviews, and commentaries, the competition of a growing number of professional and other societies, which devote a good deal of their time to contemporary issues, have all whittled away at the near monopoly of interest which the Couchiching Conference once enjoyed. Even twenty years ago, it could still win front page space in the newspaper, inspire editorial comment, and provoke letters from readers. But the period of the highest repute and widest influence was probably the first decade of its existence, the 1930s and early 1940s, when a succession of stimulating speakers from Great Britain, Europe, and the United States, as well as from Canada, faced well-informed, interested, and very articulate audiences. In those days, the Couchiching Conference was a forum for new ideas, leftish views, and exciting discussion and argument.

[The author is] indebted in the preparation of this essay for much valuable information from the following persons: Wilfred O. Smith, Dominion Archivist; David Rudkin, the University of Toronto Archives, Robarts Library; Mark Harrison, Executive Editor, the *Toronto Daily Star;* and Peter Newman, editor, *Maclean's* magazine.

Chapter Fourteen of *The West and the Nation, Essays in Honour of W.L. Morton*, Edited by Carl Berger and Ramsay Cook. Published by McClelland and Stewart, Toronto, 1976.

Perhaps the most famous of these controversies began in August 1940, at the end of the first year of the Second World War. That year the Couchiching Conference met in tragically exceptional circumstances. It had been a terrifying and demoralizing summer. In three short months, the German armies had overrun Denmark and Norway and forced the capitulation of France. In August, the Battle of Britain began with a massive and sustained air attack, which was assumed to be the prelude to a Nazi land invasion. The vast expanse of the Atlantic Ocean still separated North America from these tremendous events; but their impact was so shattering that for, almost literally, the first time, North Americans, and particularly the citizens of the United States, began to feel apprehensions about the security of what they had always regarded as their impregnable continent. President Roosevelt made two important moves, first to salvage as much as possible out of what the American administration confidently believed was the approaching defeat of Great Britain and the break-up of her Empire, and second, to organize the whole North American continent, under American leadership, for the defence of the United States. The first project ended in the exchange of fifty over-age American destroyers – most of them needed months of repairs before they could see service – for military bases, which were to be occupied without any political or social responsibilities whatever, in Bermuda, Newfoundland, and the British West Indies. The second scheme took the form of a Permanent Joint Advisory Board in which the United States and Canada would together plan the defence of North America. The destroyers-bases exchange, a complicated deal which the British accepted reluctantly, was not made public until early in September. The establishment of a Canadian-American Permanent Joint Advisory Board on Defence was announced in a press release from Ogdensburg in northern New York State, on Sunday, August 18, 1940.

Two days earlier, on Friday, August 16, the very day that Mackenzie King received his unexpected telephone call from Franklin Roosevelt, inviting him to a meeting in a railway car at Ogdensburg, the Couchiching Conference began its sessions. It was an impressive company that gathered at Geneva Park that summer. There were prominent Canadian politicians, labour leaders, and civil servants; academics from the United States, Great Britain, and Canada; diplomats, such as the Chinese ambassador to Washington and the British High Commissioner in Ottawa; and a notable group of journalists – Geoffrey Crowther from England, Geneviève Tabouis from France, and W.H. Chamberlin from the United States. The main theme of the conference, "Democracy Takes the Initiative," was an optimistic but completely unreal slogan, since the greatest western democracy was still quite unwilling, and the others utterly unable, to take the initiative anywhere against the triumphant Nazis. The speakers, even including the exile, Madame Tabouis, maintained a note of hopeful confidence through a series of sessions on politics, economics, labour, and international relations. Finally, on Friday, August 23, the last day of the conference, came a session labelled "A United American Front." This was a discussion among four speakers, two of whom, Clark Foreman of Washington and J.F. Greene of New York, were Americans. The two Canadians who made up the quartet were Dr. C.E. Silcox, a Toronto clergyman, and Professor F.H. Underhill, of the Department of History, University of Toronto.

It was Underhill's talk, supposedly twenty minutes in length, but perhaps slightly longer, which started the greatest controversy that ever grew out of the Couchiching Conference. The talk was, of course, given not from a prepared manuscript but from notes, and – a point of some importance for the future – there was no verbatim stenographic report of this or any of the other speeches. The journalists present, who knew that Underhill was always good copy and were not restricted by the precise words of a mimeographed text, simplified his ideas and sharpened his language. Underhill later protested indignantly that he had not in fact used some of the words and phrases attributed to him in the newspapers. There was an unprofitable argument over the details of his talk, but there could not be much doubt about its main purpose. It was made up of a number of the ideas which Underhill had been expressing, in oral or written form, for some years; but, on this occasion, they were delivered with a new confidence and a new fervour which, of course, had their origin in the official announcement of the Ogdensburg Agreement. Underhill was now revealed as a critic whose interpretations had been vindicated, a prophet whose predictions had finally come true.

Early in his talk, he began to emphasize the fact that Canada was now committed to two loyalties or affiliations, one of which was the old imperial connection with Great Britain, and the other the new relationship with the United States. In order to heighten the contrast between the two associations, he emphasized and exaggerated the colonial dependence and traditional adherence of the first and the independent nationalism and creative novelty of the second. In the light of Canadian external policy since 1921, it was simply not true to say that "in military and defence matters Canada had always acted as part of the British Empire and had pursued a single policy along with Britain." It was equally false to assert that the Ogdensburg Agreement came unheralded and unforeseen, when in fact it had been preceded by the Canadian-American trade treaties of the 1930s and, still more importantly, by President Roosevelt's much applauded promise of military protection in his speech at Kingston in 1938. This sharp, rhetorical contrast between the two relationships was, to a considerable extent, fictitious; but it was logically necessary, for Underhill intended to prove that the Ogdensburg Agreement had ushered a new, different, and far more natural era in Canadian history.

For Underhill, true Canadian nationalism meant detachment and autonomy in Canada's relations with Great Britain and close association and co-operation in its relations with the United States. Independence and self-sufficiency in the first case were positive and natural, unnatural and negative in the second. No assertion of Canadian nationality against the British connection was ever described as "anti-British"; but all Canada's attempts to defend its freedom and integrity against the United States were invariably characterized as "anti-American." The British tradition in government and society, the effort to develop the east-west axis of the St. Lawrence, Confederation as "a great business project . . . fenced off from American influence or interference," and Canadian reliance on British markets for wheat, were all important factors "in determining this anti-American direction of Canadian thought." This "old colonial loyalism," this economic and political dependence on Great Britain, lasted down until the conclusion of the First World War; but fortunately a better day was dawning, and during the inter-war period "a growing native Canadian nationalism" began to show itself. Canadian business became more closely integrated with American business. Exports of metals and pulpwood to the United States grew more important than exports of wheat to Great Britain. American capital, with American branch-plants and American techniques, began to take over Canadian industry.

The Second World War hastened the growth of this new North American nationality by proving that, just as Great Britain no longer provided Canada's chief markets and sources of capital, so also she could no longer act as Canada's main defence against danger from abroad. The Ogdensburg Agreement was an obvious proof of Canada's realization that her safety must depend ultimately on the security of North America: "and so we can no longer put our eggs in the British basket." Whether the British cause suffered further defeats, or whether it proved ultimately victorious, this defensive association with the United States was likely to bulk larger and larger in Canadian policy. Whoever won or lost in the end, the Second World War was almost certain to bring about a new balance of power in the world. Great continental aggregations of political and military power – a new Russia, a new Far East, a new Europe under German dominance, a pan-America from the North Pole down to the "bulge" of South America, under the leadership of the United States – these were the probabilities of the future. The order imposed by British sea power in the nineteenth century had vanished irrevocably. In the chaotic world ahead, a political anarchy like that out of which feudalism emerged, the small state would inevitably seek the protection of the nearest great power; and Canada's huge next door neighbour would become relatively a far more important factor in its existence than ever before.

Some of Underhill's ideas were expressed in arresting phrases; others, when simplified by journalistic shorthand, proved even more provocative. To some newspaper readers, "all our eggs in the British basket" sounded offensively vulgar and inappropriate in the hour of Britain's greatest danger. Others were shocked to read that "the relative importance of Britain is going to sink no matter what happens." Still others were annoyed to be informed that Canada's loyalty to North America "is going to be supreme now" and she was likely to become a mere "adjunct" to the United States. There was enough in the Toronto evening papers on Saturday, August 24, to stir up annoyance, if not indignation, in a good many Torontonians.

II

Ordinarily, the Reverend Doctor Henry John Cody, President of the University of Toronto, did not devote much time to University affairs on Sunday; but the Sunday of August 25, 1940 was clearly exceptional. The telephone at his house on Jarvis Street had rung busily on Saturday night; a number of irate citizens had complained about Professor Underhill's remarks at Geneva Park as reported in the Toronto *Telegram*. Cody was not greatly surprised, but he was distinctly annoyed. Ever since his presidency of the university had begun eight years before, he and his Board of Governors had been repeatedly forced to concern themselves with Underhill and his provocative indiscretions. He was very weary of the endless business of dealing with this apparently incorrigible troublemaker, and he determined to act decisively and at once. "Have received vigorous protests regarding report of your address in yesterday's *Telegram*," he wired Underhill at Geneva Park. "Kindly send me full statement of what you said on Friday evening." Underhill never received this telegram, for by the time it had arrived the conference was over and he had left for his summer place at Juddhaven, Muskoka; but he realized that the newspaper reports might very well have alarmed the President, and he sent him a copy of a letter he had written to the *Toronto Daily Star* in reply to an editorial criticizing his Couchiching talk. This emphatically did not placate Cody, and he repeated his request to Underhill for "a full statement of what you did say." On September 4, Underhill complied with a detailed eight-page account, from memory, of his Couchiching talk. "As nearly as I can remember," he wrote Cody, "I have reproduced my ideas as I expressed them then."

During the rest of September, while the Battle of Britain reached and passed its climax, the case of Frank Underhill continued to arouse a certain amount of discussion and argument. The members of the Board of Governors pondered what they could, and should, do in the matter, and Underhill's friends and admirers rushed to his defence. A number of prominent people, including several who had attended the famous meeting on August 23, and had heard every word of Underhill's talk, were ready to testify to its moderation and reasonableness. Principal Malcolm Wallace, of University College, the then Chairman of the Canadian Institute of Public Affairs, Norman J. McLean, who had presided over the panel discussion in which Underhill spoke, and Dr. C.E. Silcox, the second Canadian speaker on the panel, all insisted, in private letters to Cody, that Underhill's talk had not been seriously disturbing or provocative and that no reasonable man could have objected to his remarks. It was very impressive testimony; but it did not mean that liberal Toronto was united in thinking Underhill guiltless and his talk free of provocation. The *Daily Star*, to his evident surprise, considered the speech extreme and inopportune. B.K. Sandwell, of *Saturday Night*, one of the most enlightened Canadian editors of the period, who had written privately to Cody in Underhill's defence, also took occasion to rebuke him publicly in very forcible terms. "The truth is," he wrote in *Saturday Night* on September 28, 1940, "that Mr. Underhill is the most indiscreet and damaging advocate of good causes that there is in Canada. . . . It is not only unnecessary, but it is positively wrong and in these days more than positively dangerous to go around talking as if any increase in the intimacy of relationship between this country and the United States necessarily involved a corresponding decrease in the intimacy of relationship between this country and Great Britain; and this is exactly what Mr. Underhill . . . has been constantly doing for years past, and doing with particular glee in recent months."

Sandwell's comments must have awakened a responsive echo in

the minds of the members of the Board of Governors of the university. A number of them disliked Underhill's views; they disliked even more what they regarded as his offensive manner of uttering them. The majority had not yet decided what, if anything, was to be done about his case; but a minority, led by Balmer Neilly, had come to the conclusion that the university had put up with Underhill long enough and that action must now be taken against him. Neilly was a graduate of the university and a former President of its Alumni Association, who subsequently acted for years as Chairman of the Connaught Laboratories Committee and was later commemorated by the Balmer Neilly Memorial Library, a building made possible by a large grant from his own estate. He was a man in his late fifties, a highly successful mining engineer, who might have seemed the perfect exemplar of the prosperous, established, conservative, if not reactionary, industrial magnate, who in those days the provincial government seemed to regard as the ideal type of university governor. He had now been a member of the board for seven years. As Assistant to the President of McIntyre Porcupine Mines, he was in the habit of making firm decisions, and he now decided that he had had enough of Underhill. When the board met on October 11, he led the attack with a long and highly critical review of the professor's indiscretions and misdemeanours over the past few years, and ended up by moving that he be not re-engaged.

To the more liberal, or more cautious, members of the board, this proposal seemed both unwise and unconstitutional. As Hamilton Cassels, the university's solicitor pointed out, it was only on the recommendation of the President that the board could appoint, promote, or dismiss members of the teaching staff, and equitable procedure required that the President should show some cause for his recommendations. Underhill had not read a prepared manuscript at Geneva Park and no verbatim stenographic report had been made of his remarks. It would be difficult, if not impossible, Cassels reasoned, to prove that he had definitely made the provocative statements attributed to him. This objection did not seem very serious to the board members. In their eyes, the precise words spoken mattered less than the uproar they had occa-

126

sioned, and less than the fact that this rumpus was only the last of a fairly lengthy series of such disturbances. Neilly had presented a critical review of Underhill's conduct over the years as he knew it; but the board felt that it wanted something better-documented and detailed. In the end, it decided to postpone action until the President had had time "to prepare a report on the whole situation and the general record of Professor Underhill."

III

Cody's report filled thirteen closely-typed pages. In his eyes, it was a very sorry story indeed. "Since November 24, 1938," he wrote, "Professor Underhill's utterances have been discussed by the Board of Governors on seven separate occasions, including two special meetings." The board, in fact, had hardly ever stopped talking about Underhill since November 1938, and November 1938 was by no means the first time his case had come before it. Professor Chester Martin, the loyal, liberal-minded, and extremely worried Head of the Department of History, recalled that on three separate occasions in the early 1930s, he had been asked to consult with the President "in regard to Mr. Underhill's manner of discussing public questions." On the third occasion, Martin tried to establish a more permanent understanding based on a written memorandum; and the result was an interview between Cody and Underhill which, in Martin's words, was "so gratifying that we all congratulated ourselves upon the prospect of avoiding for the future any recurrence of these embarrassing incidents." For some time, Underhill "observed very satisfactorily" what Martin called "the concordat of October 1934." There were no more inflammatory speeches in public; and when, in the spring of 1939, Underhill, along with Professor George Grube of Trinity College, was suddenly denounced in the provincial legislature, it was not a talk, but a paragraph in a book which provoked the attack.

At the request of the Canadian Institute of International Affairs, Underhill had written a memorandum intended as a contribution to the Canadian submission to the International Studies Conference, which met in Paris in the summer of 1935. Although he was unaware of the fact at the time, extracts from his memorandum had been published in the report of the conference which appeared in Paris a year later; and in 1938, Professor R.A. Mackay and E.B. Rogers selected a particularly emphatic paragraph from these extracts for inclusion in their study of Canadian foreign policy, *Canada Looks Abroad*. Underhill had been asked, and agreed, to present the isolationist point of view in Canada: he did it in a style of partisan and contemptuous vehemence. The British government and the League of Nations, he argued, were bent on "alluring" Canadians into a war for democracy and freedom or peace and international order. These appeals should be rudely and peremptorily rejected. "We must make it clear to the world, and especially to Great Britain, that the poppies blooming in Flanders fields have no further interest for us." And when the "overseas propagandists" unite in a common appeal to join with them in organizing "the Peace World . . . the simplest answer is to thumb our noses at them."

Even in 1934, when these sentences were written, they might very well have seemed crude and insulting to a good many Canadians. Five years later, just after the dissolution of Czechoslovakia, when the prospect of general European war seemed frighteningly close, they looked still more obnoxious. Underhill objected that it was unfair to regard a passage written more than four years ago in comparatively peaceful times as a contribution to the anxious and fearful discussions that were going on in Canada in the spring of 1939. He complained that his few provocative phrases had been lifted out of the context of a fairly long analysis of Canada's relations with Great Britain and Europe since 1914. He went so far as to admit that a few phrases might very well have seemed offensive to people and to regret that he had used them. He even appeared before the Board of Governors and described his teaching methods in detail, explaining that he warned the students of his own biases, and tried to present all sides of a question. He was ready to explain, defend, and regret the past; but he made no precise promises for the future. "Some two years ago," he reminded the President, "I agreed with you that I would try to avoid undesirable publicity by being careful about the way in which I expressed myself in public. Of course," he went on, "I cannot guarantee that I will never at any time in the future say or write anything which, when dragged out of its context, may give someone the excuse for denouncing me as being offensive or disloyal. But I think you might take the fact that I have behaved myself reasonably well in these recent years as a guarantee that I can be trusted when I say that I shall do my best in the future to behave as reasonable men would expect a professor to behave."

This letter was written on April 18, 1939, and, in August 1940, a year and four months later, came the storm over the Couchiching talk. There were certainly "reasonable men" in the audience at Geneva Park that night who believed that Underhill had not overstepped his proper professional role; but there were others, including Dr. H.M. Tory of the National Research Council, and Brinley Thomas of the London School of Economics, who thought the talk provocative and alarming. Judgements about its character might differ, but there could be no doubt that it had stirred up a great deal of "undesirable publicity." The furor lasted so long and became so acrimonious that Underhill somewhat belatedly realized that it was doing harm to the university as well as to himself. ". . . I must obviously avoid the public platform for some time," he wrote to Cody, "and so I give you this undertaking not to make public speeches outside the University for the next year." Once again the promise was qualified, on this occasion by a limit in time. For the next twelve months – but for the next twelve months only – the university could look forward to a period of peace.

Cody had finished his report. He was more than ever convinced that this was not a question of fact about the remarks made at Geneva Park on the night of August 23, nor a question of principle over the right of free speech. It was rather, he felt certain, a question of the character and personality of a man who had shown himself to be indiscreet, provocative, and unreliable, who had failed repeatedly to live up to his gentleman's agreements and had endangered the repute of his own department and the university in the eyes of a large number of thoughtful, liberal, and loyal citizens. All this seemed demonstrably true. But what was to be done about it? If Underhill were permitted to retain his post, the troubles of the university might begin all over again, once the year's reprieve that he had granted was over. If he left the university, either through dismissal or resignation under pressure, there would unquestionably be trouble from at least a part of the teaching staff and from a good many graduates and undergraduates. Balmer Neilly, with characteristic engineering decision, had a short answer for these perplexities. "In my time," he wrote the President, "I have fired a lot of men, and the one thing I have learned is that having made up your mind, you should conclude the operation with the least possible delay." Cody and the majority of the board disagreed. They felt certain that there was a substantial difference between firing a mineworker and dismissing a university professor; and they realized that "removal" from one university might make it much more difficult to find a post in another. Resignation, they reasoned, would be a far less serious black mark on his career than dismissal, and they decided to offer Underhill a choice between the two. On January 2, 1941, a committee of three members of the board, its Chairman, D. Bruce Macdonald, Sir William Mulock, and Leighton McCarthy, met Underhill and proposed that he should either resign or be dismissed. He was given a week to make his choice.

IV

It was at this point that the opposition on Underhill's behalf began to mobilize. In the university, in Toronto, in Ontario, and over the nation as a whole, he was fairly well-known. He had a considerable number of friends, acquaintances, sympathizers, and well-wishers; and among students, graduate as well as undergraduate – although there were not a great many graduates in modern history at this time – his prestige stood very high. He had the wit, the salty style, the irreverent attitude to the great and their institutions, which quickly won the admiration of students in their early years. He also possessed the knowledge and the analytical intelligence without which the respect of senior honour students could not have been retained. Within ten days, about two hundred graduates of the university, former students of Underhill's, who were living in or near Toronto, signed a petition testifying to the stimulating quality and critical impartiality of his teaching. A large number of undergraduates, students in the various honour courses which offered modern history as an obligatory or optional subject, signed a mimeographed statement to the same effect.

With his colleagues, the professors and lecturers in history and in the Faculty of Arts and Science as a whole, his relations were different and considerably more complicated. In some ways, his position in the university was a curious one; he was in it, yet not exactly of it. He took little interest in university politics. His attendance at Faculty Council or Senate was infrequent, and at history department meetings he had comparatively little to contribute. There was, of course, nothing very unusual about this, for many scholars have been bored by university administration; but Underhill's aloofness was carried farther than that of most. He rarely sought the company of his colleagues in history, either for professional or general conversation, and he showed little or no interest in their plans for research and writing. His subjects were nineteenth and twentieth century British and Canadian history, and in these he read omnivorously; but he never attempted research or study in England and, during the 1930s, he seldom, if ever, visited the Public Archives of Canada. By 1940, when he was fifty, he had published half a dozen scholarly articles and had edited some documents for publication. On the rare occasions when he appeared at the annual meetings of the Learned Societies it was usually because some topic of contemporary and general interest was under discussion. On the other hand, he obviously gave a good deal of time to *The Canadian Forum,* whose editorial board he had joined shortly after his arrival in Toronto.

It was mainly as a popular speaker and writer, and not as a scholar, that his colleagues knew Underhill. Most of them were aware of his prowess as a teacher, his witty articles in the *Forum,* and his activities as one of the founding fathers of the CCF. He had come to be accepted as the university's "professional" radical, its apparently licensed gadfly, and there was really only one member of the university community who was totally opposed to his whole system of ideas. This was Harold Adams Innis, Head of the Department of Political Economy. Innis was, quite literally, everything that Underhill was not. They represented diametrically opposed views of what scholarship meant and what the scholar's position in the community ought to be. ". . . I imagine," Innis once admitted, "that I have crossed swords with greater violence with Professor Underhill on the platform and in print than anyone here or perhaps anywhere else." His review of *Social Planning for Canada*, a publication sponsored by the League for Social Reconstruction to which Underhill had contributed, was a characteristic expression of his contemptuous rejection of the CCF and its views. His most famous oral rebuttal was delivered at a joint meeting of the Canadian Historical and Canadian Political Science Associations at Kingston, where Underhill had scathingly attacked teaching in the social sciences in Canadian universities. With characteristically acrid wit, he denounced the economists as the intellectual garage mechanics of the capitalist system, and the historians as its white-collar promoters, who were busy selling it to the public with a slick line of talk about Responsible Government and Dominion status! Innis thought this cheap and silly. He was always sceptical about his own ability to understand the workings of the Canadian economy, and he felt perfectly certain that the cocksure Underhill had only the vaguest notion of what he was talking about. In Innis's view, it was hard enough for a scholar to keep to his true function as an objective critic of society; if he became the servant of government or party, or the slave of an ideology, the task was impossible.

Yet the news of Underhill's imminent fall moved Innis deeply; and when Professor Samuel Beatty, then Dean of Arts and Science, organized a deputation to see the President and to appeal against Underhill's dismissal, Innis readily joined in. On the afternoon of January 7, a group of about twenty people, heads of departments and senior professors from the university and University College, met with Cody in Simcoe Hall. Beatty and Underhill assumed that the President would likely begin proceedings with a sanctimonious declaration of faith in academic freedom; but, in fact, he did nothing of the kind. Instead, he gave what amounted to a brief review of his long report to the Board of Governors. The issue, he argued again, was not academic freedom, since

Underhill's real academic responsibility, his teaching, had never been impugned. The question rather, he insisted, was Underhill's character and conduct, as exhibited over a long period of time. His utterances and writings had repeatedly brought the university into discredit with the government, the press, and public opinion. He had repeatedly undertaken to behave more discreetly and had broken or explained away all his promises. What was to be done with such an unsatisfactory member of the academic community? Cody himself had no firm answer to give. He did not try to justify Underhill's dismissal. He presented Underhill's case as a problem for which some solution must be found.

The group of professors who faced the President that afternoon had only negative counsels to give. They disliked the thought of dismissal, or feared its possible consequences; but what they had to say was not an unqualified endorsation of Underhill. A few deplored his indiscreet and provocative manner. There were favourable references to his teaching ability but none to his scholarship. Beatty who, as a mathematician, was not particularly well-qualified to make a professional judgement, thought him "one of the most outstanding members of the staff"; but Flenley, one of his senior colleagues in history, also considered him "a pillar" of the department and insisted that his loss would be serious. For the majority of the speakers, the inexpediency of Underhill's dismissal, and its probably divisive effects in the university and the community, seemed more important than the iniquity of its implied denial of free speech. Innis was one of those who emphasized the undesirable publicity which would likely follow Underhill's dismissal, but the main thrust of his defence was unique. Innis, like Underhill, was a veteran of the First World War, a wounded veteran, who for years had walked with a limp and a stick. In many ways, obscure as well as obvious, this experience coloured his whole life. It left him with the conviction that the men who had endured the filth and horror of trench warfare, and had gazed repeatedly into the face of death, would never quail before any experience, however perilous, with which life might subsequently confront them. The "recklessness born of the ordeal of war" had been rooted in them all, the unwounded as well

133

as the maimed. It had driven Innis himself to extreme stands and headstrong decisions. He instinctively felt certain that it was only too likely to surge up in Underhill every time he took up his pen or faced a responsive audience. The university, he urged, must look in a special way at men who had been veterans before they became professors. "Can the University make a contribution to this war," he asked ironically, "by dismissing a veteran of the last?"

One by one, the deans, principals, heads of departments, and senior professors said their "say." Some mental reservations undoubtedly existed, but there were no dissenting voices in the appeal against Underhill's dismissal. The senior members of the university had presented a united front on his behalf; and Cody, though he apparently gave no indication of the course he and the board would finally take, must have seemed impressed. That night Beatty informed Underhill of the favourable reception the deputation had received; and next morning, January 8, Underhill wrote to D. Bruce Macdonald, Chairman of the Board of Governors, declining to resign.

V

Yet Underhill did not rely completely on the support of his academic colleagues. In this, as in many other ways, he showed that he was in the university, but not exactly of it. A large part of his life, and perhaps the part he enjoyed most, was lived entirely outside the university community. He preferred institutes which discussed current politics and international affairs to learned societies which listened to research papers. His closest friends and associates – CCFers, *Forum* editors, young publicists, and career diplomatists like Alan Plaunt, Graham Spry and H.L. Keenleyside – were all in the centre or on the edges of politics. Almost invariably he thought in political terms himself and he quickly jumped to the conclusion that the movement for his dismissal had been started by Premier Hepburn and the Provincial Government of Ontario. In actual fact, Hepburn seems to have shown not the slightest interest in the Couchiching affair; but Underhill remembered his attack in the legislature in the spring of 1939 and – which was perhaps equally important – he found it difficult to understand how people could have any but purely political reasons for wishing to get rid of him. He seemed incapable of realizing how much his provocative language and indiscreet behaviour had exasperated and wearied some of his closest associates. He himself was very quick to resent any derisive or satirical attack on his own views; and, when this happened, he would sometimes remark, his face flushing with anger, that his critic was "getting nasty." His readiness to take offence was coupled with a curious insensitivity to the feelings of others; he found it difficult to understand how people whose opinions he had ridiculed and whose patience he had tried to the limit could some day come to feel that they had had more than enough. He apparently could not conceive it possible that the President of the university, the head of his department, and all the others who, because of their official positions, had sometimes to stand between him and an angry public, would eventually come to regard him as an almost insufferable nuisance. No, the campaign against him could not possibly have originated inside the university; it must have been set in motion by outside political pressure. And political pressure could be successfully resisted only by more powerful political pressure, and never by academic appeals.

Ottawa must be invoked against Toronto! The federal government must instruct the provincial government to abandon its dangerous pursuit of the prophet of continental unity! Hepburn had undoubtedly acted in blind loyalty to the old and declining imperial connection; but King had established a new and vital relationship with the United States; and he, Underhill, was now threatened with dismissal precisely because he had publicly welcomed this new relationship and predicted its growing strength and importance. Ottawa would surely look sympathetically upon his cause; and his friend, H.L. Keenleyside, a member of the Department of External Affairs, was not only advantageously placed to forward his interests, but was also closely identified with the new policy of Canadian-American co-operation. In the anxious weeks which followed the defeat of France, when, in the judgement of the American administration, the fall of Great Britain seemed imminent, Keenleyside had acted as a confidential emissary between King and Roosevelt; and when the Canadian-American Permanent Joint Board on Defence was established in August 1940, he was appointed the secretary of its Canadian division. Underhill wrote him a hurried note on January 5, and followed it up next day with a fuller explanation of the perilous situation in which he found himself.

He could hardly have picked a more devoted advocate. Keenleyside was deeply engaged, by both sympathy and conviction, in his new task; and he acted at once with an appeal to the highest possible authority. On January 7, he drafted a memorandum explaining the Underhill case to the Prime Minister and emphasizing the undesirability of Underhill's dismissal from the University of Toronto. Underhill, he informed King, was very well-known in certain circles in the United States. He was recognized, on both sides of the international boundary, as the prophet and advocate of closer relations between the United States and Canada, and his dismissal would be interpreted everywhere as the undeserved punishment of this far-sighted advocacy. The liberal American press would give it wide publicity; the isolationists, the anti-British and pro-German elements in American society, would hold it up as a horrible example of imperialistic reaction in Canada. Its total effect on American public opinion would be deplorable, all the more so because it seemed completely to lack all semblance of justification. Underhill had not spoken in public since his talk at Couchiching more than four months previously. And if the Board of Governors took delayed action now, it might very well be with the base aim of appeasing Hepburn in the hope that he would not raise the Underhill case in the new session of the provincial legislature.

Keenleyside placed his memorandum before the chief of his department, Dr. Oscar Douglas Skelton, Deputy Minister of External Affairs, for submission to the Prime Minister. At this point, Skelton could presumably have stopped it from going further; but, like Keenleyside, he was inclined to look on Underhill as the persecuted defendant of a vital new policy in which he firmly believed, and he assumed that King might have much the same view. He forwarded the memorandum to the Prime Minister with an oblique suggestion that King, as a graduate of the University of Toronto, might think it desirable to intervene. At this point the saving of Underhill became high Liberal government policy. King later insisted that neither he nor anyone in his department – he was, of course, Secretary of State for External Affairs – had tried to persuade the supposedly angry Hepburn to call off his pursuit of Underhill. Obviously, the personal feud between Hepburn and himself, which was still very much alive, presented a serious barrier to informal communication between Prime Minister and Premier. It would have been quite impossible for King to make a direct approach himself; but fortunately there was another member of the Cabinet, C.G. (Chubby) Power, the Minister of Defence of Air, who could play the role of go-between with easy informality. A graduate of Laval University, not particularly noted for his intellectual pursuits, Power might have seemed an odd person to interest himself in the fate of Frank Underhill; but, as King saw it, devotion to academic freedom was not a main qualification for the task at hand. King was on intimate terms with Power, whom he regarded with a kind of fatherly affection; and, equally important, Power was on intimate terms with Hepburn. They had become fairly close friends when Hepburn was MP for Elgin West; they frequently corresponded with each other, and Power had visited "Mitch" Hepburn's Bannockburn Farms on several occasions. Some time on Thursday, January 9, Power picked up the telephone, called his friend Hepburn in Toronto, and asked him to use his influence to prevent the Board of Governors from dismissing Underhill. Hepburn, who up to that moment had apparently taken no interest whatever in this latest phase of the Underhill affair, promptly informed his Minister of Education, C.H. Nixon, of Power's request, and Nixon at once telephoned Dr. Cody to indicate the federal government's wish that no action against Underhill be taken at that time.

At that very moment, the Board of Governors of the University of Toronto was in session. Its members were deliberating in a state of considerable bewilderment and annoyance, for they had just received two surprising communications from the outside world of politics. The first was a telegram to Cody from Hugh Keenleyside in Ottawa; the second was the message from Power to Hepburn, which Nixon conveyed orally to the President, calling him out of the meeting to do so. Both the telegram and the message sounded the same note of urgency and used the same political argument. Underhill's dismissal, Nixon quoted Power as suggesting, would have the most unfortunate effect on the relations of Canada and the United States. "Proposed action against a man widely known in the United States as exponent of continental co-operation," Keenleyside predicted ominously, "would have most serious repercussions in that country. . . ." Keenleyside's telegram expressed earnest conviction; but Nixon, as he candidly admitted later, found it difficult to understand why Underhill was so enormously important "that his dismissal for cause could be magnified into an international incident." The President and the members of the Board of Governors shared his mystification. They were just as eager, Cody assured Keenleyside, to promote co-operation between the British Empire and the United States as any other group in Canada. "They will do nothing to make that co-operation difficult or dangerous," he added, "but I am really puzzled to see how the success of that co-operation can in any way be involved in the character and conduct of Professor Underhill." The Couchiching speech, he explained again as he had done so often before, was not the sole, or, indeed, the main cause of the board's concern. It was Underhill's indiscreet and provocative behaviour over a long period of years.

The President and the board were obviously annoyed, as well as puzzled, by this direct political intervention. On Friday, January 10, the day after the board's meeting, its Chairman, Macdonald, announced somewhat irritably to the press that if and when the board saw fit to deal with the Underhill case, it would "not be influenced by outside interests." Cody himself was equally resentful. "If and when the Board take any action," he wrote stiffly to one correspondent, "they will do so freely, according to their own judgement, and not under pressure, political or otherwise, from without." Cody was a man who had served the University of Toronto in several different capacities for a good many years and he was deeply concerned in its welfare. He was the chief guardian of the Act of 1906, which had guaranteed the university's freedom from political influence and he was convinced that the pressure from Ottawa was a serious invasion of its independence. Keenleyside and King – if the latter could ever have been brought to acknowledge his part in the manoeuvre – might have argued that their action served an important national purpose; but to Cody and the members of the board, the justification must have seemed fictitious and the interference very real. It had been prompted, moreover – though of this they may possibly have been unaware – by the very man who had made a practice of demanding academic freedom and denouncing political intervention in university affairs. And the irony of the situation was deepened by the fact that Hepburn, whom Underhill regarded as the instigator of the plot against him, became instead the agent of his deliverance.

The President and the Board of Governors maintained a sullen silence for some time. In the end, they did nothing. If Underhill was to be dismissed, the President of the university would have to recommend his dismissal, and Cody never saw fit to recommend. What had happened? Had he yielded to the pressure of that distant and alien world of federal politics? Or had he been persuaded by the appeal of the familiar and congenial community of professors and students? Or was he intimidated by what must have seemed the incomprehensible union of state and university in support of a man who had been the one serious trouble of his regime as President? In any event, he never recommended Underhill's dismissal; and the Board of Governors, after a decent interval, announced in somewhat petulant tones that it would take no action. The Underhill case was over.

VI

Underhill had won, but it soon became clear that he did not regard his victory as a splendid triumph or a complete vindication. In fact, the crisis of 1940-41 marks the beginning of a new and very different period in his career, a period much less public and sensational and much more discreet and studious than any that had preceded it at Toronto. In *The Canadian Forum* he continued to pour contemptuous and derisive abuse on anybody who happened to disagree with him; but he made no more conspicuous public appearances, and he did not provoke the Toronto newspapers or the provincial legislature into angry denunciations. His scholarly interests grew more prominent; he became President of the Canadian Historical Association for 1945-46, and was elected a Fellow of the Royal Society of Canada in 1949. His altered conduct may, in part, have been the result of an effort for greater prudence, although apparently he was not asked to make, and did not make, any promises for the future. He had come within a toucher of dismissal from the University of Toronto; and he had been saved, at the very last moment, by a man for whom he had never shown much respect or consideration. He owed a great deal to Cody, and it must have seemed obvious that he could best repay that debt, and at the same time avoid a renewal of his own danger, by behaving more discreetly in future.

Yet there was a great deal more than this in the change. It was marked not only by a more circumspect behaviour, but also by an increasingly evident shift in political loyalty. The fact was that during the 1940s the Liberal Party was coming to represent Underhill's fundamental political purposes far more completely than the CCF had ever done. From the beginning, his intellectual interests and sympathies had been much more deeply engaged in the CCF's isolationist and anti-British foreign policy than in its economic and social theories. He opposed what he always called "British imperialism" not because he was moved by a strong Canadian national feeling or even by a rooted dislike of the establishment of any kind of political and economic hegemony of one country over another. He was not a Canadian nationalist or an anti-imperialist; he fought against the imperial connection with Great Britain, but he easily accepted the imperial leadership of the United States. His real aim was North American continental unity; and, under the foreign policies of King, St. Laurent, and Pearson, this aim was coming closer and closer to realization. The Ogdensburg Agreement, which Underhill had so warmly welcomed, was simply the start of a rapidly developing trend. It was followed by Canadian-American collaboration in the Canadian North, by the hasty renewal of this alliance in the very first year of the Cold War, and by Canadian acceptance of the trigger-happy American protest against the Communist thrust in Korea and Taiwan.

Underhill's satisfaction with the post-war world and Canada's place in it was virtually unqualified. On the one hand, Great Britain was exhausted, its empire gone or going, and the ties of the Commonwealth rapidly growing weaker. On the other hand, the United States had emerged from the war as the greatest of the superpowers; its conception of an irreconcilable ideological conflict between West and East now governed world politics, and its protective alliance with Canada was obviously the dominant factor in Canadian external affairs. The Liberal Party had identified itself with those sweeping changes and had carried out the necessary re-orientation of Canadian foreign policy, and throughout the process had won Underhill's enthusiastic approval. The man who had preached against Canadian participation in the Second World War, now zealously defended Canadian involvement in the Cold War. The man who had denounced the sinister "imperialist" machinations of pre-war British politicians now extolled the moral righteousness of the foreign policy of Truman and Acheson. The extremism of his advocacy contrasted strangely with the doubts and questionings of his former colleagues or political associates. In 1947 the CCF members in the House of Commons bitterly criticized the incredible extent of the jurisdiction granted in peacetime to the American military authorities in the Canadian North. Liberals like Harold Innis and Burton Keirstead, and socialists like Kenneth McNaught, urged the wisdom of critical detachment for Canada and mutual accommodation between the superpowers. Underhill would have none of this. "There is no escaping from power politics in the present world," he declared. "And this means working in alliance with the United States. . . . Until the threat of Soviet totalitarianism has been removed, Freedom is a more fundamental issue in our world than socialism."

Ten years after the crisis over the Couchiching talk, the idea of continental unity had come to dominate Underhill's mind. To him, the North American continent was one, not only because of its close political and economic ties, but also because of its virtually identical moral values, manners, intellectual and artistic pursuits. The cultural uniformity of North America was a major principle in his social philosophy; and it was here, unfortunately, that the now exemplary Liberal government seemed to have adopted highly questionable, if not dangerously heretical, views. It actually appeared to believe that Canada possessed a distinctive cultural identity which ought to be preserved and a creative potentiality in scholarship, literature, and the arts which deserved encouragement and support from the state. It even went so far as to appoint a Royal Commission, with Vincent Massey as Chairman, which was to examine and report on the institutions "which express national feeling, promote common understanding, and add to the variety and richness of Canadian life." Underhill reviewed the Commissioner's report, and, although he praised its style and some of its recommendations, he contemptuously rejected its basic assumption that Canadian thought, art, and letters should seek to escape from the dominating cultural influences of the United States and find their own characteristic modes of expression. The idea that American social and cultural influences were "alien" was, he insisted, a ludicrous and dangerous fallacy which regrettably coloured much of Canadian nationalist thinking. "These so-called 'alien' American influences are not alien at all," he wrote, "they are just the natural forces that operate in the conditions of twentieth-century civilization."

The Liberal government may have shared some of these doubts and reservations; at any rate it waited six long years before it established the Canada Council. In the meantime, Underhill had received an appropriate reward for his devoted support of Liberal Party policies; in 1955, at the instance of L.B. Pearson, he was invited to become the Curator of Laurier House in Ottawa. Laurier House, where Mackenzie King had lived from 1922 to his death in 1950, was stuffed with the furniture, pictures, books, silver, and china which had been accumulated over the years by a man who was intensely conscious of the course of his own career and the history of his family, and who had been richly endowed by his wealthy political associates and friends. Laurier House had, in fact, become a shrine to both the King family and the Liberal Party, with William Lyon Mackenzie King as the central deity of both, and Underhill as his attendant priest. Along with R.M. Dawson, the author of the first volume of the Mackenzie King biography, Underhill could now be accepted as one of the "official" scribes of the Liberal Party tradition. Moreover, he did not simply regard himself as the guardian of the heroic Liberal past; he was also ready to fight for the Liberal future. In the federal general election of April 1963, he wrote a series of campaign pieces for the *Toronto Daily Star.*

The apotheosis of Underhill as the great spiritual leader of twentieth-century Canadian liberalism came with the dinner which celebrated his eightieth birthday. It was held at the Rideau Club in Ottawa, and was very much a Liberal establishment affair. There must have been well over a hundred diners. A few old associates in the founding of the CCF were there; but the later leaders of the party, and of its successor, the NDP, were conspicuous by their absence. Most of the academics present came from those two faithful strongholds of Liberal thought, Queen's and Carleton University; and there were several representatives of the federal civil service, that unofficial but powerful arm of the Liberal Party. These were the intellectuals who had helped to build the one-party Canadian state, whose convictions, loyalties, and antipathies had taken concrete shape in the reality of modern Canada. They were aging now, but they had finished their work and were well satisfied with it. Their former leader, L.B. ("Mike") Pearson, who had done so much to realize Underhill's continentalist foreign policy, appropriately made the first of the laudatory speeches; and Underhill responded with a bland air of conscious political virtue and acknowledged political success. "I simply cannot understand the view prevalent today," he declared to his delighted audience, "that there is something vicious about the Liberal establishment." The happy diners laughed their agreement. They were established, secure, and complacently comfortable in the prospect of the indefinite prolongation of Liberal rule.

Harold Adams Innis:
A Special and Unique Brilliance

Some little time ago, the head of one of the University of Toronto's new colleges put a sudden and very general question to me. What, he said in effect, is the importance of Harold Innis? I must admit that I was surprised and slightly annoyed by this abrupt inquiry and I made no serious attempt to answer it. I might have replied that Harold Innis had been the Head of the Department of Political Economy and the Dean of the Graduate School, that his published works in history and political economy numbered more than a dozen, that he had sat on several Royal Commissions, and that his advice was almost invariably sought, during a large part of his career, on every important university issue and appointment in Canada. I might have made an answer along these lines, but I decided not to. I was repelled by the idea of summing up Harold Innis in what would have sounded like a short paragraph out of *Who's Who*. Besides, I could not help suspecting that my questioner was not likely to be much impressed by any brief answer I might make. His inquiry was not an honest request for information, but a disguised expression of disbelief. He probably knew very little about Innis and his works, and he was not disposed to accept the Innis legend on trust. He rather brusquely invited me, a friend and a known admirer, to justify my faith in it.

It seems to me that this little incident makes a point, or raises a question of some importance. Has the time come for a re-

---

Under the title "Harold Adams Innis: An Appraisal," this was the keynote address of the Innis symposium held at Simon Fraser University, in March 1978.

examination, a re-interpretation, even a re-appraisal of Innis and his work? The twenty-fifth anniversary of his death occurred early last November, and frequently this particular anniversary prompts a critical backward look at the work of a formerly popular author or prominent scholar. Harold Innis deserves such a retrospective review as much as any Canadian scholar and more than most; but the twenty-fifth anniversary came and went unmarked by any special effort at commemoration. The University of Toronto Press at first planned to publish a memorial volume of essays in his honour; but in the end this project fell through, and only my own short biography, *Harold Adams Innis: Portrait of a Scholar,* was reissued in paperback. This absence of a special remembrance was perhaps unfortunate; but it by no means implies a decline in the high evaluation of Innis's work. The very existence of this symposium, which takes place over half a continent away from the city where he lived and wrote, is in itself a significant proof of the enduring vitality of his ideas. And in Toronto, the Innis Foundation, which for some years devoted itself to the task of converting the old Innis farm into a study and conference centre, has now returned to its original and main purpose, which is the encouragement and promotion of studies about Innis and his ideas.

II

It would be difficult to think of another Canadian scholar whose stature equals or approaches that of Harold Adams Innis. Banting won a knighthood and the Nobel Prize. Wilder Penfield has been, so far, the only non-political Canadian to become a member of that highly select body, the British Order of Merit. But these brilliantly creative scientists and medical men left behind them no great body of written work for the instruction and delight of their fellow Canadians. Harold Innis did, and the very bulk, as well as the brilliance, of that work forces upon us the difficult but fascinating task of investigating the origins of the complex mind that conceived it.

The farm, on which he was born and grew to manhood, and the First World War, in which he almost lost his life, were the two most important early influences in his life. Both were to have important and permanent after-effects; but the farm – the home – and the Baptist faith and morality which pervaded it, were probably basic and primary. It was a complex, varied influence, and Innis's own attitude to it was extremely ambiguous. He hated its stultifying labour and was only too glad to escape from it for ever; but he never forgot its seasonal rhythms or its complex daily operations. It taught him also, for his father's farm was a relatively poor one, the need and practice of hard work; and throughout his entire academic career, he was repeatedly forced to increase his small income with student teaching. The farm gave him the directness and simplicity of his approach to people and things, his insatiable interest in significant detail, his capacity for hard, sustained labour, and his enormous powers of endurance.

It also exercised, through the religious and cultural interests of the farm household, a direct and powerful influence on Innis's standards and values. The Innises were Baptists, "hard-shell" Baptists, their neighbours called them, who believed in adult baptism by total immersion, and who lived a simple, narrow, and devout existence. Innis had not yet undergone the formidable rite of baptism when he left Otterville to join the Canadian army; but he was still a professed Christian, and he told his sister solemnly that he did not believe he would have volunteered if it had not been for his Christian faith. How much of that faith survived the horrors of the First World War is uncertain; but certainly there was none of it left in his later years. He had ceased to be a Baptist; but he clung tenaciously to certain convictions and values which have always been characteristic of his sect. He believed in the independence, dignity, and self-sufficiency of the individual; and he utterly rejected any compromise with his high standards in scholarship or teaching. Many people, when they are angered by an unjustified slight, or an unmerited favour to others, go as far as to threaten resignation. Harold Innis didn't threaten to resign; he just resigned. He resigned when a junior was appointed over his head in the Department of Political Economy at Toronto, and he withdrew his resignation only when he was promoted to the same higher grade in the academic hierarchy. Years later, at the height of his career, he angrily resigned from the Royal Society of

146

Canada on the ground that one of its awards had been bestowed on an unworthy fellow; and the academic world of Canada was confronted by the astonishing spectacle of one of its most distinguished members openly boycotting the proceedings of its most prestigious society!

There was still another important but negative influence of the Innis household, its undeniable cultural poverty, which, in my view, profoundly affected Innis's development. The *Family Herald* was the only periodical that arrived regularly at the farm; no metropolitan newspaper entered the home until Innis, who, like the rest of his family, was then a stout political Liberal, subscribed to the Toronto *Globe*. His family's speech was slovenly and ungrammatical; and Innis learnt his first big words from reading Borden's and Laurier's speeches on the Naval Bill in the House of Commons. There may have been a small library in the farmhouse, but, if so, its existence is not recorded. The young Innis no doubt gulped down a good many books; but they were books which, in the main, bore directly on the academic courses he was taking at Woodstock Collegiate Institute or McMaster University in Toronto. Even at McMaster, he never seems to have plunged into that fascinating debauch of extracurricular reading to which so many undergraduates succumb. At McMaster, he was known not as a bookworm, but as a debater, a powerful opponent in intercollegiate debates. And his success made him think of law as a career.

It was not until a good deal later, when Innis went to Chicago and fell in love with Mary Quayle, that he became dimly aware of this great, gaping hole in his general education. Mary Quayle was, as she later proved, a writer herself, and very well-versed in modern and contemporary English literature. During her engagement with Innis, she lent him a novel by Willa Cather, the leader of an early twentieth-century group of midwestern novelists in which she was interested. Innis later admitted that he had read the book, but had, if I remember correctly, nothing whatever to say about it; and if the loan of Cather's *My Antonia* was intended to start him off on an extended course on the modern novel, it was a total failure! Years later, when Harold and Mary visited our Muskoka cottage, I tried to create a diversion from endless academic gossip, by reading some of the pieces from Stephen Leacock's *Nonsense Novels* or *Sunshine Sketches of a Little Town*. Innis was immensely amused and laughed uproariously, but it was obvious that this was the first time he had encountered Leacock. He had never even heard his name before!

Years later, in a series of lectures on prominent Canadian historians and economists, which was sponsored by the Departments of Political Economy and History at Toronto, Innis gave a paper on Stephen Leacock. With laughable professional complacency, he attributed the vividness and accuracy of *Sunshine Sketches of a Little Town* to the fact that Leacock was an economist! In the entire history of English literary criticism there is probably no more hilarious absurdity than this inept remark. It was Leacock's inspired novelist's insight into the characters and circumstances of his little town – the gift of a born storyteller – and not the laboriously acquired knowledge of an economist which gave his *Sunshine Sketches* their freshness and authenticity. What Harold Innis badly needed – and what he never took the trouble to acquire – was a thorough knowledge of the realistic and naturalistic novelists, French and English, of the nineteenth and early twentieth centuries. A thorough course of reading in Balzac, Flaubert, Zola, in Trollope, Bennett, and Galsworthy, would have shown him clearly how far novelists excel economists in depicting the social circumstances and class relationships of a given country and period.

There is one last major formative influence on the development of the early Innis – the First World War and its effects – which remains to be explored. When he left the family farm in South Norwich township to join the Canadian artillery, Innis had felt himself to be a Christian soldier engaged in a holy crusade; when he came back, war had, for him, turned into a monstrous, sickening mixture of blood, filth, and stench. His experience left him with an enduring sense of sympathy and comradeship with the men who had actually risked the peril of front-line fighting; but for everybody else supposedly engaged in the war, he had nothing but uncompromising contempt. As an economist, he might have been expected to realize that modern warfare was a vast, complicated enterprise in which thousands of non-combatants played essential parts; but, in fact, he was even more unwilling to apply Adam Smith's dictum about the necessary division of labour to the Second World War than he had been to the First. In his view, non-combatants were simply bureaucrats, who risked nothing and battened on the war's emoluments of money, prestige, and power. Bureaucracy meant regimentation and centralization and all the other evils of big government which Innis instinctively hated. And the Second World War, directed and controlled by a triumvirate of war lords, was an even more monstrous example of centralization. Innis simply endured it. He watched young university teachers go off to Ottawa, or London, or Washington, without interest and with barely concealed contempt. In his opinion, their real place was in their universities, guarding the threatened traditions of scholarship.

III

For Innis, the First World War was a horrible but comparatively brief interlude in a life increasingly devoted to academic study. He had refused to take advantage of McMaster University's dubious offer of a free degree to fourth-year students who enlisted before the end of the year, and had stayed stubbornly on to write his examinations. In June 1917, when he was stuck in the trenches at Vimy, and there appeared not the remotest prospect of his release from fighting, he wrote to McMaster University, asking for information about the requirements for the M.A. degree. A month later, a severe wound in his knee took him back to England and eventually to the Canadian General Hospital at Basingstoke; and there he started in to read the formidable list of books which Professor Duncan McGibbon had provided him and to write an M.A. thesis on his own chosen subject, "The Returned Soldier." He reached his home at Otterville at the end of March 1918; and within only two days he was back again in Toronto, conferring with McGibbon. There was time for only a last fortnight of frantic study, and on April 19, he wrote his examinations. Only a few days later, he was honourably discharged from the army; and on April 30, in

Walmer Road Baptist Church, McMaster University's Annual Convocation awarded him the M.A. degree.

It was an astonishing record, carried out in an incredibly brief space of time. In only a little more than six months, a convalescent soldier, distressed by occasional periods of pain and weakness, had shown extraordinary powers of grim determination and compulsive speed. He had passed all the barriers now, academic and military; he richly deserved a holiday, but now, as always, he was in a hurry. There was the problem of his future career. In vain his mother renewed her old pleas that he become a Baptist clergyman. He himself had vaguely considered the law as a profession, and now he finally decided upon a legal career. His professional training at Osgoode Hall in Toronto was to begin in September 1918; but before that happened, there were five empty months to be filled in. Most young returned soldiers, if they had been academically as far advanced as Innis, would have welcomed a summer of comparative idleness, but Innis was not among their number. He discovered that the University of Chicago, to which McMaster was accustomed to send its most promising students for further study, had a graduate summer school. He decided to attend.

That summer at Chicago was decisive for Innis in a number of very important ways. A course in economics, given by Professor Frank Knight, completely absorbed him, so much so that by the end of the summer he had made up his mind that he would work for a doctoral degree in economics at Chicago, and seek an academic career as a teacher in that subject. He was launched on the study of Canadian economic history through the choice of his thesis subject, the Canadian Pacific Railway, and through an elementary course in economics, which he taught at his supervisor's request, he met, and soon fell in love with, one of his students, Mary Quayle.

There was no doubt whatever about a job, for in both Canada and the United States the veterans were returning to their studies, and universities all over the continent were busily recruiting staff. A variety of academic openings were available, but Innis wanted to teach in Canada and preferred a senior and recognized university.

Very quickly his hopes were realized, for Toronto offered him a position as lecturer in economics at a salary of two thousand dollars a year. In the autumn of 1920, he began to teach in the Department of Political Economy, and in the spring of the following year, he married Mary Quayle.

Obviously, the first definite period in Innis's academic career begins with his appointment at Toronto in 1920, is neatly bisected by the publication of *The Fur Trade in Canada* in 1930, and ends with the appearance of *The Cod Fisheries, The History of an International Economy,* in the early winter of 1940. For both Innis and his chosen subject, economics, it was a period of rapid advance and steady enlargement. In 1937, when he had been only seventeen years in the department, he was appointed its head. Those seventeen years witnessed an amazing increase in the range and depth of Canadian studies in economics. The revival of the Canadian Political Science Association in 1931 was followed four years later by the founding of the *Canadian Journal of Economics and Political Science.* The publication of the two-volume *Select Documents in Canadian Economic History*, edited by Innis and Arthur Lower, gave students for the first time an opportunity of getting at the roots of their subject. The launching of those two large scholarly enterprises, *Canadian Frontiers of Settlement*, edited by W.A. Mackintosh, and *The Relations of Canada and the United States*, edited by James T. Shotwell, gave senior scholars in Canadian economics, history, political science, and sociology more opportunities for publication than they had ever had before.

In contrast with the second period of Innis's career, which began in 1940, the first was essentially Canadian, North American in character. It was not, of course, that he carefully avoided contact with England and Europe. During the 1920s and early 1930s, he made perhaps half a dozen trips to England and the continent, chiefly in the guise of an economic geographer, which was the academic role he liked to assume at the time. He attended geographical conferences and made an investigation of German methods of teaching geography; but he never stayed very long, never did any serious research in England or Europe, and never attempted to learn a European language. By an odd coincidence, I encountered him myself on one of his brief European visits. In the summer of 1928, I was working at the Bibliothèque Nationale on a subject in French revolutionary history. At that time Innis and I knew each other only slightly; but he showed a friendly interest in my researches, and we went out together for a light luncheon, which probably consisted, as mine invariably did in that summer of abject poverty of *"un sandwich au jambon."* I remember that as we passed the guardian at the gate of the library, he muttered the one word *"retourner."* I never heard him speak a sentence or even a lengthy phrase in French. He may have come back again to the library, as he told the guardian he would, but I never saw him again that summer.

The brevity and infrequency of these European visits provide a striking contrast with the steady and unflagging zeal with which he explored Canada. The famous journey down the Mackenzie River in the summer of 1924 was only the most exciting and dangerous of his many travels. In those first ten crowded years at Toronto, he could be said to have realized the motto of the Canadian coat-of-arms: "He shall have Dominion from sea to sea, and from the river unto the ends of the earth." He became intimately acquainted with the land, its regions, resources, and industries. He got to know its universities, their principal scholars, and promising juniors. Through J. Bartlet Brebner, who had left Toronto for Columbia University, he became acquainted with James T. Shotwell, one of the directors of the Carnegie Endowment, and through him with Joseph Willits and Anne Bezanson of the Rockefeller Foundation, and Henry Allen Moe of the John Simon Guggenheim Foundation. These influential American associations were vital to Canadian scholarship in those days, for the establishment of the Canada Council was decades in the future. I had gone to Paris in 1928, on my own meagre savings; but in 1940, I won a Guggenheim Fellowship, through, I am sure, the influence of Harold Innis.

The fact that Innis became a power in Canada and a potent influence in the United States was the result mainly of the two major works which he produced during this period, *The Fur Trade in Canada* and *The Cod Fisheries, The History of an International*

Economy. Both these books were applications of what came to be called the staples approach to Canadian economic history. Innis was not the sole inventor of this approach; but in the final chapter of *The Fur Trade in Canada* – which was one of the strongest chapters he ever wrote – he gave the classic exposition of the general theory upon which the staples approach was based. The migrant to a new country like Canada, he assumed, was desperately dependent for the maintenance of the culture he was accustomed to on the importation of manufactured goods from his homeland; and for these he could pay only by the discovery of a native commodity or staple which was available in fairly large quantities in the colony, which was light enough to be carried for long distances in the little ships of the period, and which was either unknown or scarce, and consequently desirable, in the Motherland. For Canada, the first two of these staples were fish and furs.

The *Fur Trade* and the *Cod Fisheries* are excellent examples of the way in which Innis carried out the application of this theory to Canadian economic history. His method of composition was unusual, highly distinctive and, at times, extremely exasperating. A large amount of the task of understanding his books was left to the reader. He insisted on including large chunks of original documents, in an undigested, and sometimes almost indigestible form. All too often his sentences were awkward collections of words, with a series of huge abstract nouns, connected by a few rather feeble and frequently repeated passive verbs, carrying the main action of the narrative or the chief burden of the argument. This dense, leaden exposition might go on for paragraphs, or even pages, when it could be suddenly interrupted by a brilliant generalization, or a short paragraph which simply but superbly summed up pages of exposition, or a final chapter which suddenly seemed to open up vast horizons of understanding to the reader.

In those exceptional features of his work, the *Fur Trade* is surely the better of his first two books. Perhaps he tired in the end of the endless involutions of the story of the fisheries. Perhaps the sheer weight of his material overwhelmed him. At any rate, the vast untidy manuscript which he finally sent down to New York was too much for James T. Shotwell, the general editor of the series *The Relations of Canada and the United States.* He succeeded in persuading Innis that considerable revision was essential; and Arthur W. MacFarlane, an old friend of Shotwell's, came up to Toronto and for more than a year worked with Innis over the revision. It was he who supplied the appendix to Chapter Two, which explained the coins and money values of the period – a complicated subject which Innis had majestically ignored.

Innis's uncompromising attitude to his readers had its origin in his conception of economics. He believed that it was a science, a difficult science certainly, with serious limitations which invited study and exploration, but definitely precluded any final, dogmatic conclusions. No word appeared more frequently in his work – it was part of the title of one of his collections of essays – than the word "bias." No man was ever more acutely aware of the fact that everybody – including the most supposedly detached economist – was a creature of his own generation and environment and deeply affected by its values, assumptions, and beliefs. Such arguments, carried to their logical extreme, could end only in complete relativism; they could mean only that an objective economic science was logically impossible. This absolute conclusion Innis refused to accept. Bias was the social scientist's greatest danger; but paradoxically it was also his best hope of salvation. Biases, he seemed to say, are an historical phenomenon which is always with us and can be studied and analyzed just like any other historical phenomenon. And through such study the economist could discover the cumulative force of biases, and their effect on institutions.

This was a modest defence of economics as a difficult science without dogmatic conclusions. It also provided a useful retort to the radical reformers of the 1930s, who suddenly appeared as a result of the world's worst depression, and who were always demanding drastic economic or political changes and insisting that economists should direct and aid the politicians in carrying them out. The League for Social Reconstruction – the very name was abhorrent to Innis – was founded early in the 1930s; the first Canadian Socialist Party – the Co-operative Commonwealth Federa-

154

tion, with a manifesto stuffed with huge economic and social generalizations – followed shortly after. Innis had nothing to do with either of these organizations. He dealt with them only when he was attacked by one of their members, or when the League for Social Reconstruction produced a book, *Social Planning for Canada,* which purported to be a serious intellectual exposition of its socialist principles. Innis gave this pretentious effort a highly critical review in the *University of Toronto Quarterly*; and a year later at the first meeting of the revived Canadian Political Science Association, when F.H. Underhill denounced the Canadian economists as "the intellectual garage mechanics of the capitalist system," and urged them to throw aside their timid academic scruples and join the holy crusade for a socialist Canada, Innis made such a devastating reply that thirty-five years later, George Ferguson, the editor of the *Montreal Star* was still marvelling over it!

For Innis all social planning on the grand scale was bad; but the social planning proposed by the Canadian socialists was particularly bad because it assumed the federal government as the chief agent of social change. In sharp contrast with today, when a chorus of pious Canadians propose to save Confederation by pulling it to pieces or cutting it up into shreds, the constitutional reformers of the 1930s were all strong federalists. It was their federalism almost as much as their socialism which aroused Innis. He had nothing to do with the great federal Doomsday inquiry of the 1930s, the Royal Commission on Dominion-Provincial Relations. The only economic investigation of the 1930s in which he took part was Nova Scotia's Provincial Economic Inquiry of 1934; and even here he was careful to assert his own intellectual independence. The two other commissioners signed the main report. Innis wrote a separate report, a complementary report he called it, which was mainly an economic history of Nova Scotia, with a few, relatively small specific recommendations tacked on.

IV

The second and final period in Innis's career started with the real beginning of the Second World War in the spring of 1940 and the commencement of his researches in the history of paper, printing, and the press in the summer of the same year. This second period, which lasted only twelve years, differed markedly from the two decades which had preceded it. The range of Innis's work grew vastly larger and more ambitious. Before his studies had been largely confined to North America; now he seemed to appropriate the whole world and travel freely up and down the centuries of its history. He became much more deeply involved in the economic, political, and social issues of his time than he ever had been before; and his criticism took on a much more pessimistic and intransigent tone. He had always dealt occasionally in generalizations and epigrams. Now the generalizations grew more frequent and sweeping, the paradoxes more daring, the conjunction of ideas and the relationship of events more unexpected and startling.

It seems to me that it is possible to explain the later Innis – the angry, gloomy, obscure, and overconfident Innis of the post-war period; and that the explanation is to be found partly in the radical change in his own researches and partly in the revolutionary transformation of the post-war world itself. It is difficult for the historians and political scientists who now occupy the senior positions in Canadian universities to appreciate the profound impact which this revolutionary transformation in world affairs had upon Innis. He lived through it all. He witnessed the British Empire's last desperate effort and the beginnings of its rapid decline. He saw the rise of the three great new empires which were to dominate the post-war world – the United States, the Soviet Union, and the Republic of China. Canada, he realized, was passing inevitably from the light and easy obligations of an old empire to the uncompromising orders of a new one. During the war, this control took the form of an armed occupation of the Canadian North by American forces, virtually uncontrolled by the Canadian government. During the peace it changed into a heavy diplomatic pressure which forced Canada to support American imperialistic policies in the Far East and eventually took us into the Korean War. The United Nations, under peremptory American direction, justified the Korean War; and in those days Lester Pearson and the Canadian Department of External Affairs regarded the United

Nations as a divine institution, created by God for the preservation of collective security and peace. And looking back now, after a lapse of nearly thirty years, we can realize how wonderfully correct they were in their confident expectations, can't we? In their eyes, the Korean War was a noble crusade for the collective system. Innis saw it for what it was, an American imperialist war decked out in a pious cloak of United Nations respectability!

These profound changes in world politics affected Innis deeply; but there was another important influence – the scope and nature of his new research – which also radically altered his outlook. Originally, pulp and paper had no doubt been conceived as another study of a Canadian staple industry, not unlike the fur trade and the fisheries; but, as time was to show fairly quickly, it was, in fact, radically different. The fur trade and the fisheries had fairly definite limits in time and place; but once Innis had passed from pulp and paper to printing, the press, and communications generally, he had entered an almost illimitable field. Communications was an open-ended subject. It stretched back into remote historical times and forward into the present and future. It was an enormous, monstrous subject; and the fundamental difficulty that Innis faced in tackling it was that he was almost as ignorant of the immediate present as he was of the remote past. He was no great newspaper reader, found little interest in popular periodicals, rarely listened to the radio, and, of course, never saw television. His ignorance of Latin and Greek was more abysmal than his unfamiliarity with French; and it is probable that before the early 1940s he had barely heard of the Greek poets, dramatists, and philosophers whom he quoted so freely in the fourth chapter of *Empire and Communications.*

Inevitably, the new, vast work which he had undertaken forced him to adopt new methods which differed radically from the old. In the past, his work had always been based on a careful study of the available documentary evidence and on comprehensive knowledge of the geographical setting. Now, neither one of these solid foundations could possibly be built. It was just as impossible for him to gain a detailed knowledge of the geography of Europe and the Middle East as it was for him to acquire an intimate acquaintance with the world's modern journalism. He had no time to turn himself into a Greek or Roman historian or an Egyptian archaeologist, and he could not spend his life reading daily newspapers. What he read, in fact, was *not* daily newspapers, or Greek philosophers and dramatists, or Latin historians, but books *about* them. Every night he arrived home with a bulging briefcase. He gulped down books like a man dying of hunger and thirst. He devoured what to other scholars would have been whole libraries.

As he worked, a theory rapidly developed. The *Fur Trade* and the *Fisheries* had both produced a system of assumptions, which had come to be called the staples theory; but the staples theory applied only to colonial times and to limited areas. The new communications theory which Innis now rapidly elaborated was far more grandiose in conception; it was both global and eternal in its significance. The media of communications, he came to believe, were the central factor in the history of organized society; and changes in the character of the media meant alterations, often drastic, in institutions, social organizations, and cultural values. Two main classes of media had existed from the beginning of time, each with its different qualities and influences. A heavy, durable medium, such as stone, clay-baked tablets or parchment, emphasized stability, permanence, or time. A light, easily-transported material like papyrus or paper meant rapid dissemination over distance or space. A medium of communication which favoured time, he believed, emphasized local initiative, respect for antiquity, and religious observance. A space-based medium encouraged secular attitudes, centralized, bureaucratic government, imperialism, and technocracy. Like Oswald Spengler and Arnold Toynbee, Innis was attempting to explain the rise and fall of civilizations, the growth and collapse of empires; but unlike Toynbee and Spengler, who found complex explanations, laden with diversified historical evidence, Innis relied on a simple mechanical determinant, expressed in the twin categories of space and time. He did not openly predict the downfall of western civilization, as both Spengler and Toynbee had done, but from the angry despair with which he wrote of modern times, we can hardly doubt of what he believed its inevitable end would be.

158

In June 1946, Innis received a letter from the administrators of the Beit Fund at Oxford University, inviting him to give six lectures on any subject in the economic history of the British Empire. Innis had nothing new that he wanted to say about the economic history of the British Empire; but he was burning to deliver himself of the great new theory of communications which had been maturing rapidly in his mind for the last few years. The Beit lectures were given two years later, in the Trinity Term of 1948; but even before that, Innis had crammed the substance of his great new theory into his presidential address to the Royal Society in the spring of 1947. In the next few years, he seemed to proclaim it everywhere. He lectured at the University of Nottingham and the University of London; he gave the Sesquicentennial lectures at the University of New Brunswick. In the last six years of his life, four books of his essays and lectures were published. It was as though he was driven by a desperate compulsion to deliver his last message to a sick and troubled world. And then, the cancer, which was to end all these efforts for ever, began inexorably to destroy his life.

He was that rarest of all beings in Canadian history, a genius – not a flawless and immaculate genius, but a genius whose characteristic weaknesses and imperfections, the flaws of his upbringing and training, seem almost to heighten and intensify his special and unique brilliance.

John Bartlet Brebner:
A Man of His Times

North Atlantic Triangle, The Interplay of Canada, the United States, and Great Britain is John Bartlet Brebner's most characteristic book, and, for that very reason, probably his best. It is not, as Brebner himself made clear in his preface to the first edition, a work of original research. He was, of course, quite capable of a very high level of original scholarship; and his two books, *New England's Outpost* and *The Neutral Yankees of Nova Scotia*, are, without any doubt, two of the most important books on the history of Canada that have appeared during the twentieth century. Yet it was something of an accident that an "Upper Canadian" born and bred should have begun his career as an historian with a book on Nova Scotia. At that time, Brebner was a young scholar, not yet thirty years old, who had begun teaching in the Department of History at the University of Toronto. He wanted to start serious research and to gain a senior degree; and in teaching Canadian history he had become curious as to whether the experience of the British with the Acadians in Nova Scotia had given them any guidance in approaching the problem of the French Canadians in Quebec. At this point, he was simply searching for a promising subject, in the normal fashion of post-graduate students. But the work which finally appeared as *New England's Outpost, Acadia Before the Conquest of Canada*, was certainly not a normal doctoral dissertation.

Published as the introduction to the Carleton Library edition of *North Atlantic Triangle* by John Bartlet Brebner. McClelland and Stewart, Toronto, 1966.

It was, in fact, a quite remarkable book which, in its undemonstrative but penetrating fashion, cut cleanly through the thick layers of myth and sentimentality in which the subject of the Acadians had previously been wrapped. Not surprisingly, many good critics in Canada and the United States praised the book and urged its author to pursue his researches into the history of this mysterious frontier peninsula, with a study of Nova Scotia's inexplicable course during the American Revolution. In the end Brebner yielded to these flattering entreaties and the result was *The Neutral Yankees of Nova Scotia, A Marginal Colony During the Revolutionary Years.* He had given some of his best years to Nova Scotian history, and in the process had gained a number of Maritime friends and acquaintances and acquired a large stock of knowledge of Maritime history and public affairs. But at this point, as he made quite explicit in the preface to *The Neutral Yankees,* he left the subject to others.

The two books on Nova Scotia formed a part, an important part, but a part only, of his whole experience. *North Atlantic Triangle* may be regarded, not extravagantly, as an epitome of his entire career. Many, if not most, university people are migratory for at least a part of their lives; but Brebner crossed international boundaries more frequently and for a longer period than the vast majority. In the end he became what might appropriately be described as a citizen of the English-speaking academic world; and he began his career as a wandering scholar at an age earlier than was then considered possible by even the most adventurous. The elder son of a father, who for a great many years held the post of Registrar at the University of Toronto, he grew up in a particular university atmosphere; and since he showed himself from the first to be a brilliant student, he might very naturally have been expected to live his life out there. But strangely enough, as things turned out, he never got even his bachelor's degree from Toronto. His graduating year was 1917, and like a great many Canadian students who would have graduated in the fated middle teens of this century, he went overseas to fight in the First World War. A large number of these soldier students never returned to Canada; but of those that did, many resumed their studies at Canadian universities. Brebner was not among them.

Instead he won an exhibition at St. John's College, Oxford, and began to read the Modern History school. There he gained his Bachelor of Arts and Bachelor of Letters degrees. But unlike a few other young Canadian scholars in somewhat similar circumstances, he did not remain in England. The University of Toronto was then passing through the first, and smaller, of the two great post-war expansions it has experienced; and at the invitation of Professor George M. Wrong, the Head of the department, Brebner became a lecturer in history. He had returned to very familiar academic surroundings and seemed to have settled down; but those of his contemporaries who pictured his gradual ascent up the hierarchy at the University of Toronto were wrong. He taught only from 1921 to 1925 in the history department at Toronto; and he then accepted an offer to join the staff in history at Columbia University, New York City.

There was nothing very unusual then about this kind of academic emigration, though perhaps it happened rather less frequently to historians than to teachers in other disciplines in the sciences of humanities. Very many of these emigrants became almost completely absorbed, sooner or later, in a life which in many important ways was very like that which they had left; and, apart from occasional sentimental journeys back to the land of their birth, they ceased to concern themselves about Canada. But here again Brebner, though a migratory Canadian, was an unusual Canadian emigrant. His teaching responsibilities and interests were mainly in Canadian and British history; his writings were on Canadian, and, to a much lesser extent British, themes. He spent the rest of his professional career at Columbia University; but for a long time he kept in very close touch with Canada, and, in the latter part of his life, he recovered his old contacts with England. In the years before and during the Second World War, he frequently visited Canada, often attended the annual meetings of the Canadian Historical Association and the Canadian Political Science Association, kept up an elaborate correspondence with a large number of Canadian scholars, and became an extremely well-informed and influential authority in Canadian university affairs. After the war, and partly as a result of the publication of his widely praised *North Atlantic Triangle,* he resumed and greatly extended his old relations with academic life in England, though this time through Cambridge, not Oxford University. Cambridge appointed him Pitt Professor of American History for the session 1954-55; and for the duration of his tenure he became a fellow of St. John's College. He spent a good deal of time at St. John's during the late 1950s, including the last summer of his life.

It was a wide, varied, and absorbingly interesting experience, and very early in his passage through it, Brebner was moved to ruminate and speculate on its significance. He had been an intimate part of three distinct political expressions of twentieth-century English-speaking civilization. A sensitive and reflective person, he was constantly aware of the similarities and differences, of the associations, attractions, and repulsions that existed among them. He began to want to make comparisons, to point out contrasts, and to speculate about their origin and meaning; and fairly early in his career at Columbia University, this new interest found expression in occasional, rather casual essays and papers. In 1931, six years after he had gone to Columbia University, two of these short pieces appeared: one, called "Oxford, Toronto and Columbia," and published in the *Columbia University Quarterly*, was a comparison of the three universities in which he had studied and taught; the other, entitled "Canadian and North American History," was a paper delivered to the Canadian Historical Association at its annual meeting in May 1931.

Obviously the essay on higher education in the English-speaking world had a broader scope than the paper on Canadian and North American history. The first compared a Canadian university with universities in both the United States and the United Kingdom; the second concentrated on Canada and its position in the North American continent. Within its limits, "Oxford, Toronto and Columbia" suggested in a general way the fashion in which Brebner's interests would ultimately develop; but "Canadian and North American History" foreshadowed quite accurately the course which his scholarly studies would follow for more than the next decade. This second paper was a very characteristic production of Brebner's, heavily freighted with references to books and articles from a wide variety of sources, and full of allusions to the researches and ideas of other historians and economists. Its purpose, as Brebner pointed out in the first section, was to urge Canadians to change their point of view and broaden the frame of reference in which they studied their history. "The procedure of matching contours, or of merging the local in the general, is of course," he argued, "particularly applicable to neighbouring societies." It followed therefore that "the method of applying North American, that is, continental, contours to the histories of Canada and the United States" would probably prove to have very valuable results. What these results might be for Canadian history Brebner then proceeded to discuss. He pointed out basic similarities between Canadian and American history; he noted important differences. Throughout the paper, however, ran the implicit assumption that these suggestions were merely tentative and provisional, and that the method of "matching contours" in North American history would yield really valuable results only if historians, economists, political scientists, statisticians, and sociologists united in a massive attack upon the subject as a whole. "Canadian and North American History" hardly pretended to do more than sketch the possibilities of its theme. It suggested a new method – the continental approach to Canadian history. It adumbrated an enormous programme of research.

Scholars occasionally toss off such ambitious proposals. Sometimes the proposals reach the stage of elaborate planning; but often they go no further. Brebner was one of the few historians who have lived to see a suggestion of a great co-operative work completely realized. The paper that he read to the Canadian Historical Association at its meeting in Ottawa in the spring of 1931 was the direct inspiration of the long series of volumes which were published by the Yale University Press and the Ryerson Press under the general title of *The Relations of Canada and the United States*. The fact that this huge project was begun and finished within little more than a single decade is, of course, astonishing; but, in the light of existing circumstances, it is less astonishing than it appears at first sight. Brebner was very closely and sympathetically in tune with his times. He expressed an attitude which was very fashionable at the time; he indicated an approach that was likely to prove very congenial to many Canadians. Moreover, he had influential connections in places of power. His friend and mentor in New York was James T. Shotwell, Director of the Division of History and Economics, in the Carnegie Endowment for International Peace.

In some ways, Shotwell was a Brebner of an earlier generation. A Canadian, who had also gone to the University of Toronto and had been taught history by Professor Wrong, he had come down to Columbia University for post-graduate study and had eventually become a member of its staff in history. In later life, Shotwell liked to describe himself as "an academic casualty" of the First World War. He had originally intended to become a medieval historian; but his irrepressible interest in contemporary problems and international affairs found wide scope and opportunity in the negotiation of the peace settlement, and the creation of the League of Nations. He was appointed Chief of the History Division of the American Commission to the Paris Peace Conference, 1918-19; and thereafter he played a large part in a number of commissions, societies, and conferences concerned with international affairs. He gave up some of his academic duties at Columbia in order to join in the direction of the Carnegie Endowment for International Peace; and from that vantage point he began to inspire and promote a number of scholarly projects which had international understanding and conciliation as their object. At the moment when Brebner read his paper on "Canadian and North American History" to the meeting at Ottawa, Shotwell had just completed the editing of a great series of volumes on the economic and social history of the First World War. He was ready for a new and large undertaking; and, as a former Canadian who had lived most of his life in the United States and thought of himself as a citizen of North America, he quickly saw the great possibilities of Brebner's idea and was powerfully attracted by it. He decided to take on the publication of a series of volumes on Canadian-American relations as a project of the Carnegie Endowment.

Brebner had found his sponsor. He was also encouraged by an enthusiastic response from the very scholars whose support he had hoped to enlist. The "continental approach" to Canadian history was not so novel as he had imagined; but it had never before been so fashionable as it was in the 1930s. "You and I differ widely in our general views," Goldwin Smith had once written to John A. Macdonald. "You regard Canada as a part of the British Empire, I as a community of the New World." Macdonald might very well have replied that Canada was both, and that the two views of it were historically perfectly compatible. He would not have persuaded Goldwin Smith, that patron saint of all Canadian continentalists; and he would equally have failed to convince the much less intellectually able continentalists of the 1930s. In 1931, these people could hardly help but believe that history was on their side. Mackenzie King's heroic crusade for what used to be called "Dominion status" was about to be completed and crowned by the passage of the Statute of Westminster; and the continentalists hailed this joyfully as the modest Canadian equivalent of the great and glorious American War of Independence. Canada, now that the malign domination of Great Britain had been removed, could respond more freely to the dictates of nature. She could become more openly what she had always been in reality, a typical North American community, virtually indistinguishable from the United States, governed by the same forces, and destined to pass through an almost identical historical experience. All that Canadian historians and social scientists had to do, in order to understand Canada, was to keep their gaze firmly fixed upon the North American continent, to examine Canada's relations with the United States, to assess the influence of the Republic upon the Dominion, and to investigate the parallel historical movements in the two countries.

Yet, strangely enough, the series *The Relations of Canada and the United States* never quite became that imposing and integrated demonstration of continentalism that some Canadians may have expected. The continentalists never dominated the enterprise so completely as they may have hoped. Some of them much preferred the exhilarating exercise of talking or dashing off short, sophomoric pieces to the more exacting labour of writing books. Others made the sad discovery, when they began to assemble the evidence, that their studies, judged by strict continentalist canons, were likely to prove disappointingly unorthodox. As they dropped out or failed to respond, their places in the series were taken by other and rather different scholars, many of whom were recruited by Harold Adams Innis, the Head of the Department of Political Economy at the University of Toronto who, on Brebner's recommendation, had been invited to supervise the volumes concerned with the economic aspects of Canadian-American relations. Innis had little belief in continentalism; in fact, his second book, *The Fur Trade in Canada,* went far to demolish the geo-political bases on which continentalist theories were founded. Moreover – and this was equally important – Innis did not believe that a series ought to be organized in a rigid fashion or that definite specifications ought to be laid down for each volume, as if it were a subcontract in the construction of a large block of apartments. Every scholar of any ability, he was convinced, had already fixed upon some subject from which it would be criminal to divert him; and the task confronting the editor of a series was therefore to discover what volumes were being written, and to publish the best of them, provided they could be shown to have some plausible relation to the project in hand. As a result, *The Relations of Canada and the United States* is a somewhat unsystematic series, with a few unaccountable gaps and some dubious inclusions.

As it progressed, the character of the series changed and shifted. It had been conceived and started when North American isolationism seemed certain to dominate Canada's future; it was finished when all divisions of the English-speaking world were united in fighting a gigantic and terrible war. In 1931, when Brebner had read his paper to the Canadian Historical Association, Great Britain and, indeed, the whole of Europe, seemed to many Canadians to have receded so far into the distance that they had become mere specks upon a very remote horizon. Ten years later, in 1941, the forgotten islands and the forsaken sub-continent had rushed backwards so swiftly and so overwhelmingly that they seemed to fill the entire sky. A decade before, Great Britain had been regarded by complacent North Americans as quite unworthy of any special effort on their part; now the fate of the whole of western civilization appeared to be bound up with Britain's survival. The brute force of events altered the world outlook of a whole generation of North Americans; and Brebner, who was very much a man of his times, changed with them as well.

To him the lesson of the years 1939-1944 was plain. In both his paper on "Canadian and North American History" and in the plan for the series *The Relations of Canada and the United States*, there was, he felt, an enormous omission. He had left Great Britain out. He had assumed, like the continentalists, that North America was self-sufficient and that the history of the United States and Canada and of their relations with each other was self-explanatory. This assumption, he now recognized, was mistaken. North America could not be explained in purely North American terms. Canada in particular could not be understood without constant and copious reference to Europe in general and Great Britain in particular. It was too late now to alter the character of the series in the light of this realization. But several of its published volumes had already served to modify and correct the original simple thesis; and Brebner decided that his own contribution would carry an even more explicit admission of the central deficiency of the series. From the beginning, he had planned to write a book of his own which, while it could not be and was not intended to be a summary of the other volumes, would nevertheless present a general view of the subject as a whole, or of most of its important aspects. That book must now, he realized, be redesigned in order to place Canada and Canadian-American relations in their true setting.

The very title of the volume as it finally appeared, *North Atlantic Triangle, The Interplay of Canada, the United States and Great Britain,* was in itself a statement of his altered conception. His preface defined his original purpose, and admitted the failure of his original method. "My primary aim," he wrote, "was to get at, and to set forth, the interplay between the United States and Canada – the Siamese Twins of North America who cannot separate and live. By interplay I do not mean merely the manifestations in what are usually called international relations, but the various kinds of things which the peoples of the two countries did in common, or in complementary fashion, or in competition. . . . The great obstacle to a simple account of this interplay was that many of these activities could not be explained in merely North American terms. Most notably of all, the United States and Canada could not eliminate Great Britain from their courses of action, whether in the realm of ideas, like democracy, or of institutions, or of economic and political processes.''

This was the justification of the book's subtitle, *The Interplay of Canada, the United States and Great Britain*. The subtitle seemed to imply that each of the three members of the triangle would be given equal treatment; but in his preface Brebner candidly admitted that he "had felt forced to give Canada more attention than her importance relative to the United States and Great Britain would ordinarily justify. . . ." This emphasis on the weakest and most subordinate member of the partnership was explained on the ground that the author "could not count upon any large amount of common knowledge" concerning Canada. The inadequacy of material on Canada was, of course, even more obvious then than it is today; but it hardly seems a complete explanation of the bias of Brebner's book. A full and satisfactory account of the interplay of the three countries would inevitably have given Canada a very minor, and even marginal, position. But in Brebner's thought Canada was not marginal. She was still central. His interests were still concentrated upon her, as they had been in almost everything he wrote. And the real purpose of his book was to place Canada in the external circumstances which he believed had influenced her most.

This, which is the book's basic idea, is also its most novel feature. Brebner himself claimed no more. In his preface he observed that he had had to depend more upon the research work of others than upon his own; and this was necessarily true, though in several respects his own books had prepared him very effectively for this new task of synthesis. His *The Explorers of North America* had given him a very comprehensive and detailed knowledge of North American geography. He had learnt a great deal about North American population movements from the time and effort he had given to the completion and editing of M.L. Hansen's *The Mingling of the Canadian and American Peoples*. His friendship with Harold Innis had helped to increase his appreciation and knowledge of Canadian economic developments; and the several volumes in the Canadian-American series devoted to the diplomatic relations between the two countries provided him with a large mass of material on which to draw. On the subject of political ideas and institutions, on the other hand, the series gave very little guidance; and here, perhaps, for that reason, *North Atlantic Triangle* was also weak. Canadian Confederation would seem to offer a most rewarding case for the study of the inter-action of political ideas and forces; but Brebner's treatment of the subject is conventional and somewhat perfunctory; and like R.G. Trotter before him, he exaggerates the importance of the activities of Edward Watkin, and the other agents of British "financial imperialism."

North Atlantic Triangle is a very "busy" book. It is packed with a mass of very detailed information about a wide variety of subjects; and in these respects it is very characteristic of the breadth of Brebner's interests and of the frequently great particularity of his knowledge. He was, in fact, a very knowledgeable man. He read constantly and widely. He was a good conversationalist with a fine "Senior Common Room" manner; he enjoyed gossip. Nothing pleased him better than a long, intimate discussion with some recognized authority or expert from which he would carry away quantities of confidential, recondite, and esoteric information for use with telling effect on subsequent, more public occasions. His curiosity was unending, his experience was wide, his sympathies were generous; and he observed men, events, and opinions with an air of bland omniscience. *North Atlantic Triangle* is not his most original book; but it is the book that sums up his career and expresses his interests and his qualities most completely.

Charles Perry Stacey: Intellectual Independence and the Official Historian

Charles Perry Stacey, the son of Dr. Charles Edward Stacey and his wife, Jennie Margaret Perry, was born in Toronto in 1906. His forebears on both sides were Irish Protestants, who came from the southern counties of Tipperary, Wexford, and Kilkenny, and the county Down. The Perrys immigrated to Upper Canada in the early 1830s and for two generations worked farms in York and Ontario counties. The immigrant Staceys, who arrived a generation later in the middle 1850s, had, from the start, a more varied history in the country of their adoption. William Stacey, Charles Perry Stacey's paternal grandfather, had taught school in Ireland, but failed to find a teaching post in Canada, and, after some experience as an itinerant merchant, opened a general store in Fleetwood, Durham County. He soon became the Fleetwood village postmaster and in 1858 was commissioned ensign in the Fifth Battalion of the Durham Militia. His military interests, which foreshadowed his grandson's vocation, were a revealing indication of the basic political convictions which the Staceys and Perrys held in common. Richard, the first Canadian Perry, who lived in the region from which William Lyon Mackenzie drew his strongest support, stoutly opposed the Rebellion of 1837, and William Stacey, new to the agitated politics of mid-century Canada, looked doubtfully at Clear Grits and advanced Reformers. Like so many other Irish

"Charles Perry Stacey," from *Policy by Other Means, Essays in Honour of C.P. Stacey*, edited by Michael Cross and Robert Bothwell, published by Clarke, Irwin and Company Limited, Toronto, Vancouver, 1972.

Protestant immigrants, the Perrys and Staceys were Anglican in religion, Conservative in their political sympathies, and warmly loyal to Great Britain and the imperial connection.

Charles Edward Stacey, William Stacey's son, was the first member of the family to fit himself for a professional career. He received his training at the Trinity College Medical School and, after some years' practice at Acton, Ontario, he decided to try his luck in Toronto. In 1898, when he was forty, he married Jennie Margaret Perry – she was invariably called "Pearl" by her intimates – and in the following year, they established themselves in a three-storey red brick building at 161 College Street. It was there that their daughter Dorothy and son Charles Perry were born. The children grew up in a district which was rapidly becoming a part of old Toronto, in the centre of the largest academic foundation in the Province of Ontario. Only a little way from their parents' house, up what is now King's College Road and across the front campus, stood University College. Victoria College, St. Michael's College, and that excellent collection of books, at the Toronto Public Reference Library, as well as some of the oldest and most esteemed schools in the city, were all within easy walking distance. Charles first attended that venerable institution, the Model School, on Gerrard Street. Later, he was transferred to the University of Toronto Schools, "U.T.S." as it was familiarly called, which had already established a considerable reputation.

In 1923, when he was seventeen, Charles Stacey entered University College, the non-denominational college in the University of Toronto, whose façade had been so familiar to him since his earliest years. He enrolled in the honour course in English and History, then one of the strongest and most popular courses in the Faculty of Arts, a course which had been designed by Professors W.J. Alexander and G.M. Wrong and included languages, as well as English literature and British and European history, in its programme. Modern History, in accordance with the division of subjects between the colleges and the university in Toronto's federal system, was a university subject. Languages ancient and modern, as well as classical history, belonged to the colleges. Charles had the benefit of the scholarship and teaching ability of both University College and the Department of History and, in the middle 1920s, each had a great deal to offer him. University College was in the midst of one of the most distinguished periods in its long existence, and in the early post-war years, George M. Wrong, the dean of Canadian history, had gathered about him a group of young and very talented associates. At University College, the Department of English Language and Literature, with veterans like Alexander and Malcolm Wallace and gifted newcomers like Herbert Davis and R.S. Knox, was an exceptionally strong teaching department. W.S. Milner in classical ethics and politics was an erudite teacher with a fine speculative mind, and Charles M. Cochrane in Greek and Roman history was a scholar of great creative power. In the history department, George M. Smith, Hume Wrong and J. Bartlet Brebner were sympathetic tutors and brilliant lecturers who quickly communicated their enthusiasm to their students.

Charles Stacey's career at University College was busy and varied. Each year, he gained first-class honours in his course; he won scholarships and prizes, including the All Souls Historical Prize, awarded for a substantial essay on a set subject. His academic record was consistently excellent, but this high standing was not bought by any narrow concentration on academic study. Charles was interested in military training, student theatre, and journalism. He joined the Canadian Corps of Signals, in the Non-Permanent Active Militia, in 1924, and was commissioned a year later. He became a member of the University College Players Guild, where he got to know his future wife, Doris Shiell, and was elected its president in his final year. He early began writing for the *Varsity*, the undergraduate newspaper, and, in the session of 1926-27, took on the exacting job of editor. "In its editorial policy," the *Torontonensis* of 1927 commented, "the *Varsity* has attempted to escape the lower and less interesting forms of lunacy" – an aim which, of course, would appear incredible to the psychotic student leadership at Toronto in recent years. The *Varsity* certainly occupied a great deal of his time, but did not adversely affect his standing; and, in 1927, when he graduated with first-class honours, he seemed an almost certain prospect for a

Rhodes Scholarship. Unfortunately, his plans for his own future did not exactly coincide with the career which the Rhodes examining committee had projected for him. The committee saw him as an influential newspaper editor; Charles knew that he wanted to teach and write history. He missed the Rhodes, but in the autumn of 1927, he left for Oxford and Corpus Christi College, on a scholarship founded in memory of Sir George Parkin, the first secretary of the Rhodes Trust.

At Corpus Christi, where R.B. Mowat, a frequent writer on British foreign policy, was his principal tutor, Charles read the Modern History school. His second Bachelor of Arts degree, which he gained from Oxford in 1929, did not now satisfy him. He wanted the directed training in historical research and writing which only a good graduate school could give; and it was fortunate that at this important stage in his career he won a fellowship to Princeton University. Princeton gave him the expert guidance of such scholars as Professor T.J. Wertenbaker and Professor R.G. Albion; it also brought him into direct and intimate contact with still another great university and with the best in the intellectual life of a great neighbouring power. In these encouraging circumstances, his basic historical interests developed quickly, and he soon fixed upon the subject, Canadian military history, which became the major occupation of the rest of his career. He first chose the Fenian movement in the United States and the Fenian raids on Canada as the subject of his doctoral thesis. This theme led him into a general study of Anglo-Canadian military policy and practice in the 1860s and early 1870s, and when he discovered that Fenianism had already been pre-empted as a thesis subject by another graduate student, he was able to alter the main emphasis of his dissertation with relative ease. It now became a study of the military relationships between Great Britain and Canada during the period from the fall of the old Colonial System to the recall of the imperial garrisons in 1871.

In the meantime, during the first years of his graduate study at Princeton, he began to publish. His early essays, which appeared in such varied publications as the *Canadian Historical Review*, the *Canadian Defence Quarterly*, the *Queen's Quarterly*, and the

Dalhousie Review, were mainly concerned with Canadian defence during the Rebellion of 1837, the American Civil War, and the Fenian troubles. The most ambitious of them, "Fenianism and the Rise of National Feeling in Canada at the Time of Confederation," which dealt with what would have been one of the main themes of his projected thesis on the Fenians, was printed in the *Canadian Historical Review* for September 1931. Less than two years later, he finished his dissertation, the Department of History at Princeton accepted it, and he gained his senior research degree. It was the spring of 1933, the nadir of the Depression. Openings for young historians who hoped to become university teachers were rare enough throughout North America, and virtually non-existent in Canada. For a year he taught in an academy in Long Island, New York; but Princeton remembered him, and in 1934, he joined its staff as an instructor in history. Despite the large demands which the first years of teaching made upon his time, his essays continued to appear, and in the winter of 1935, he completed the revision of his thesis. It was published in that same year as a volume in the series *Imperial Studies* edited by Professor A.P. Newton, with the title *Canada and the British Army, 1846-1871, A Study in the Practice of Responsible Government.*

In the Canadian circumstances of the later 1930s, Charles's subtitle *A Study in the Practice of Responsible Government* was charged with meaning. Only five years earlier, the Statute of Westminster had granted "Dominion status." Mackenzie King had succeeded in liberating Canada from the sinister coils of imperial defence and foreign policy, and for an entire generation, Canadian historians had been celebrating the heroic struggle by which the nascent Canadian nation had won full autonomy from a reluctant and stubbornly-resisting Great Britain. In the prevailing intellectual climate of the time, Charles's first book might have appeared on the surface as a set of new and interesting variations on an old and very familiar theme. In fact, of course, it was an abrupt departure from both the subject matter and the historical approach which had been popular in Canada for the previous quarter-century; in several important ways, it anticipated the lines along which Canadian historical writing would develop during the quarter-century that followed. Charles's major interest was Canadian military history, and one of his major themes was the relations of Canada and the United States. The older liberal historians, obsessed with the problem of the imperial connection and the struggle for "Dominion status," had virtually ignored these topics, but in the decade that followed the publication of *Canada and the British Army*, they became steadily more popular. The war years produced a group of able military historians, many of whom further investigated this field. The final pre-war years saw a revival of Canadian interest in the United States, and the growth of the idea that Canadian history could best be understood in a North American or continental frame of reference. During the late 1930s, the first volumes in that mammoth series *The Relations of Canada and the United States*, edited by James T. Shotwell of the Carnegie Endowment for International Peace, made their appearance. For a while the continental approach threatened to supersede the imperial approach to Canadian history.

Professor J. Bartlet Brebner, who first conceived the idea of the Shotwell series, had been one of Professor Wrong's gifted young lecturers of the early 1920s, and had left Toronto for Columbia University. He gave Charles friendly advice and encouragement during the gestation of *Canada and the British Army,* and invited him to contribute a volume, called tentatively *Armament and Disarmament in North America,* to the series, *The Relations of Canada and the United States.* To a considerable extent, the two men – Brebner was Charles's senior by eleven years – shared a common experience and a common outlook. They were Canadians who had enjoyed the privilege of an intimate knowledge of both a great British and a great American university, and they had come to know and appreciate the values and best qualities of the two greatest nations in the English-speaking world. Bartlet Brebner, who became an American citizen, and Charles Stacey, who remained a British subject, both saw their subjects in the context of the North Atlantic world. Brebner had originally planned to make his own contributions to the Shotwell series, a study of "the interplay of Canada and the United States"; but in 1945, when the book finally appeared, it bore the title, *North Atlantic Triangle, The Interplay of Canada, the United States and Great Britain.* Brebner had come to realize that the United States and Canada could not be explained apart from Great Britain. Charles Stacey had always assumed that Canada and Great Britain could not be understood apart from the United States; and his *Armament and Disarmament in North America* would probably have served as a companion piece to *Canada and the British Army.* He was and remained devoted to Canada and its history; but he was always conscious of the claims and interests of its neighbours and relations, and he wrote about their associations and encounters with cool detachment and unemotional clarity.

Late in August 1939, Charles Stacey married Doris Shiell, a graduate in the honour course in Modern Languages at the University of Toronto, whom he had met when they were students at University College. Only a fortnight later, Canada entered the Second World War. Charles had kept up the military contacts which he had formed as an undergraduate at Toronto. At Oxford, he had been attached to the University Officers Training Corps, and with the 3rd Divisional Signals (Royal Corps of Signals), had taken part in Southern Command Training at Salisbury Plain. His name had remained on the reserve list of officers in the Canadian militia throughout his ten years at Princeton, and, when the war broke out, he naturally assumed that he might soon be called up to serve as a brigade signals officer in the Canadian Army. However, the army had other plans for him. Charles went back to Princeton in September 1939, and again in September 1940. He busied himself in writing a series of articles on the first phases of the war for the *University of Toronto Quarterly,* and in working on a study which was published in 1940 as *The Military Problems of Canada: A Survey of Defence Policies and Strategic Conditions, Past and Present.* He might have remained at Princeton for the duration of the war if it had not been for an acquaintance with Brigadier H.D.G. Crerar, who at that time was Commandant of the Royal Military College at Kingston. During his honeymoon, Charles called on Crerar and consulted him about his study on Canadian military problems. Crerar left for England that autumn, but he did not forget Charles. He was determined that the deeds of the Canadian Army should be properly recorded, and in the summer of 1940, when he returned to Canada as Chief of General Staff, he moved quickly to establish an overseas representative of its Historical Section. Early in October, he offered Charles an appointment as a historical officer, with the rank of major, in Canadian Military Headquarters, London. Charles accepted immediately. He spent some time in Ottawa acquainting himself with the operations of the existing Historical Section, and sailed from Halifax on the troop freight ship *Capetown Castle*. He landed in England on Christmas Day, 1940.

He was superbly fitted, by choice, training, and historical approach, for the great task he had undertaken. He was a commissioned officer, who was quite prepared to work within the familiar framework of the army. He was a professional historian who was accustomed to assume responsibility for everything he wrote and who was determined to insist on his intellectual independence. He was not to escape the conflict implicit in every "official" history – the conflict between official control and historical truth – but for him a valid and acceptable reconciliation of the two existed. His job, as he saw it, was to elicit the facts and to state them fully and frankly; and this was not a conclusion imposed upon him as a requirement of his new official status, but an assumption deeply rooted in his instinctive method and natural habit of mind. He had already proved that he wrote history without personal prejudice or nationalist bias; his work had never been organized according to preconceived theory or built up with imaginative reconstructions or coloured for dramatic effect. Precision, clarity, economy of words, and strict impartiality were already established features of his historical approach.

His first task was to find and collect the facts. Indeed, that was all he was authorized to do by his letter of appointment. He was not yet an official historian; his duty was to assemble and prepare material for an official historian yet to be appointed. At first, and for a long time, he worked alone; it was not until the autumn of 1942 that his first assistant, George F.G. Stanley, joined him in London. By the following summer, when the invasion of Europe at last began, with the Canadians as part of the assaulting forces, the little historical enterprise which he had started began rapidly to expand. The staff in London was steadily enlarged. A historical officer and a war artist – the latter a suggestion of Vincent Massey, the Canadian High Commissioner in London – were appointed to each Canadian division in the field, and there were also officers established at Corps and Army Headquarters. With historians such as Stanley, J.B. Conacher, G.W.L. Nicholson, Eric Harrison, T.M. Hunter, and S.H.S. Hughes, and war artists like Charles Comfort and Will Ogilvy, it was a highly talented company, some of whose members remained to take part in the arduous business of writing the history and others who went on to fine careers in the universities and at the bar.

Yet in the autumn of 1944, when the war was already drawing to a close, the whole future of Charles's project was still veiled in obscurity. Masses of material had been collected; preliminary narratives had been written; but what form the history was to take and who was to write it were still undecided. The political and military authorities in Ottawa and London seemed uninterested in answering these questions, and since Charles was anxious to see his great work take concrete shape in a set of volumes, he had to take the initiative himself. The history, he thought, should be written for the "intelligent general reader," and therefore it could not be technical and ought not to be too long. He planned, on a modest scale, for a history proper in four volumes to be preceded by a preliminary one-volume survey or sketch which would tell the whole story of the Canadian Army's war effort. He was ready to act as official historian and to direct the whole undertaking if proper conditions could be secured, and he knew very clearly what these conditions must be. The official historian must be given full access to all official material; his responsibility for all "references drawn and opinions expressed" must be accepted and there must be no censorship by the Department of Defence; and the completed volumes, when recommended by the official historian, should be subject to the approval only of the Chief of General Staff and the responsible minister. These were, of course, the irreducible stipulations required to safeguard the status and reputation of a professional historian. Charles was prepared to insist on them. At the back of his mind was the comfortable reflection that if these essential requirements were denied and a valid army history became impossible, he could always go back to the work he knew and liked in a Canadian or American university.

For a while it seemed certain that he would be given these indispensable assurances. In those first post-war years, when Canada's pride in its war effort was at its height, most of Charles's programme looked very acceptable. The plan for a four-volume history with a preliminary one-volume sketch for early publication did not appear inflated or ostentatious, and there could be no serious rival to Charles for the post of official historian. With a prescience remarkable for one still relatively unused to the devious ways of Canadian politicians, Charles obtained approval for his plan from both A.G.L. McNaughton and Douglas Abbott, the first two Ministers of Defence with whom he had to deal, and in the autumn of 1945, he was appointed Director of the Historical Section of the General Staff, as well as Official Historian of the Canadian Army in the Second World War. For an anxious moment, it looked as if the pledge of no censorship and the guarantee of historical truth might be qualified or denied. Briefly, uncompromisingly, General McNaughton asserted the principle of official control; but his tenure of the defence portfolio was brief, and subsequently General Foulkes, the Chief of Staff, gave Charles assurances which quieted his fears for the honesty and completeness of his history. He and his colleagues plunged into the first part of their programme, the preliminary sketch or summary of the Canadian Army's part in the Second World War.

They were well on their way to its completion when the shattering blow fell. In December 1946, Mackenzie King reorganized his cabinet, and Brooke Claxton, a large, shambling, inept man, with a high-pitched, grating voice, became Minister of Defence. Claxton, who had taught law at McGill University, and was admiringly regarded by his colleagues as an "intellectual," had decided that, after the first few post-war years, no Canadian would have the slightest interest in histories of the armed services, and the drastic opinion of this "scholar politician" was apparently more than enough to convince the Liberal ministry that stopping war histories was one of the best possible ways of cutting expenditure. The naval and air force stories, Charles was informed, were to be brought to a stop immediately. The one-volume preliminary sketch of the army history, perhaps slightly enlarged, might be completed; but the rest of Charles's publishing programme would have to be dropped. After the early spring of 1948 – little more than a year away – no more money was to be spent on war histories.

Charles saw Claxton, reminded him that two former Ministers of Defence had approved his plan for the army history in detail, and bluntly charged the Liberal government with breach of faith. He was prepared to resign and to seek an academic post, preferably at Queen's University. The fact that in the event he did not do so has its explanation not in any spontaneous change of mind on the part of Claxton or the cabinet as a whole, but in the completely fortuitous intervention of an outside influence which awakened the Defence Minister to the enormity of the deed he was about to commit. George Brown, a Professor of History at the University of Toronto who was in Ottawa on other business, paid a visit to his friend R.G. Riddell of the Department of External Affairs who, like his Deputy Minister, L.B. Pearson, had taught history at Toronto. Together they called on Pearson, and the Deputy Minister of External Affairs mentioned casually, as if conveying a mildly interesting piece of gossip, that the war histories were to be dropped. Brown at once expressed astonishment and dismay, informed Pearson firmly that this was a most deplorable decision, and prophesied that Charles was certain to resign. Pearson, who had apparently not given the matter a moment's serious thought up to that point, telephoned Claxton and put Brown's argument forcibly to him. Within forty-eight hours, the government's decision was substantially changed. It was not completely reversed, for the naval history was never finished, and the story of the air force, which had been tentatively planned on a most ambitious scale, was not begun until many years later. But the army history was saved.

With the help of a powerful external influence, Charles had won his first battle with the politicians. An equally serious engagement now confronted him. A history was to be written on the scale that he had planned, but its completeness and historical truth had yet to be assured. Both the Chief of General Staff and the Minister of Defence would have to approve the publication of the volumes; and although Charles expected, and met, no serious difficulties with the soldiers – who believed in honest history, even of their own failures – he encountered prolonged resistance and obstruction from the politicians. Claxton, who was acutely sensitive to the political implications of almost any statement about contemporary affairs, and who was obstinately determined to save the Liberal Party from the slightest reflection on its political virtue, was evidently shocked by the candour of Charles's narrative. Ralph Campney, who succeeded Claxton as Minister of Defence, was almost equally perturbed by the frank and detailed record set down without reserve or extenuation. Claxton, who imagined that he could teach Charles style as well as political discretion, made copious critical comments on the one-volume preliminary sketch or summary; but when, in the latter part of 1953, he received the first two volumes of the history proper, he must have realized with horror that their fearful political revelations could hardly be veiled by mere textual amendment. Faced with such an irremediable situation, he simply did nothing; he reserved approval for publication; and Ralph Campney, his successor, followed the same policy of masterly inactivity. Campney was apparently reluctant even to discuss the history with Charles. He repeatedly suggested, and repeatedly postponed, an interview.

It was not until the summer of 1955 – well over two years after he had sent the manuscript of the first volume to Claxton – that Charles finally decided that he had had enough. At luncheon in the University Club at Ottawa, in the company of several members of the Department of National Defence, he angrily declared that if Campney did not grant him an interview before leaving for the summer vacation in British Columbia, he would resign from the service, sacrifice his pension, and tell the story of his neglect and ill-usage to the Canadian people. Although Charles was not aware of the fact, one of his startled auditors at the luncheon was close to

Campney and repeated this outburst to him. Two days later, Charles got his long-postponed interview with the Minister of Defence; and a month later, the cabinet decided to publish the history without official editing or censorship, on the principle that the historian had been given free access to all official material but that the interpretation and commentary were his own. It was exactly the same principle that Charles had set out in his original proposal in the summer of 1945. The King and St. Laurent governments had taken ten years to recognize its validity.

Once the roadblock of official fear, distrust, and inertia was removed, the publication of the history went steadily forward. *Six Years of War,* the first of Charles's two contributions to the series, was published late in 1955, and the second, *The Victory Campaign,* the story of operations in northwest Europe, appeared four years later. "The volumes," their author wrote much later, "were written in a studiously low key, consciously unsensational and unprovocative in tone. . . . This was the way I thought official history should be written." It was also the way in which he preferred to write history in general. His manner had not been adopted to meet the special requirements of a governmental task: it was his own manner, the natural and instinctive manner in which he approached and dealt with any historical problem. He did not try to back away from the mistakes, failures, missed opportunities, and controversies – including the famous controversy between Montgomery and Eisenhower over the broad or narrow front – which marred the record of the Allied armies as a whole or the Canadians in particular. He did not seek to avoid the contentious subjects which all too frequently evoked personal prejudice or national bias in other historians. He dealt with all such issues in a cool, detached, dispassionate fashion, which remained realistic and critical, without ever becoming evasive or non-committal.

In 1959, the year in which *The Victory Campaign* was published, Charles Stacey retired from the army and joined the staff of the University of Toronto, first as a special lecturer and, after a year, as Professor of History. He had been in the army for nineteen years, but the army history of the Second World War had never been his only interest, and he had kept up his contacts with the academic world. For three months in the winter of 1948, when Professor R.G. Trotter was ill, Charles went down to Kingston for several days each week to take his classes. This brief return to undergraduate teaching was not, however, the only, nor perhaps the most important, of the many ways in which he kept in touch with his old colleagues and abreast of new developments in historical studies in Canada. He was President of the Canadian Historical Association, 1952-53, and Honorary Secretary of the Royal Society of Canada, 1957-59, and these posts brought him into close association with a number of Canadian scholars. He continued his regular contributions to the learned journals, and only during the last years of the war was there any serious interruption in the steady continuity of his reviews. He had always been an indefatigable reviewer, dealing with books of general interest as well as specialized military studies, and now the war and the army history had greatly extended the range of his interests and his competence. He was able to judge and evaluate the war histories and memoirs which flooded the book market in the early post-war years with an expertise which no other Canadian could have equalled.

Yet his chief interest remained Canadian military history. The huge demands of *Six Years of War* and *The Victory Campaign* left no time for a general history or large specialized studies; but substantial articles on a wide range of themes continued regularly to appear. Charles had always looked with a very sceptical eye at historical myths and legends, and some of his most characteristic work of the 1950s was devoted to exposing the favourite fables of Canadian and North American history. Too many Canadian historians had jumped too easily to the gratifyingly patriotic assumption that it was really the Canadian militia, not the British regulars, who had saved Canada in the War of 1812, and too many Canadian and American politicians and publicists had fostered the complacent assumption that the War of 1812 had seen the last of conflicts and quarrels, real or apprehended, between Canada and the United States; that henceforth the four thousand miles of undefended and peaceful frontier had been a symbol of North America's will to peace and a reproach to Europe's insatiable appetite for war. In a paper which he gave to the Ontario Historical Society in 1958, Charles quickly cut the ground from under the "Militia Legend of 1812." The Canadian militia, he told his audience, played an essential but secondary part in the war; the regulars supplied the leadership and "usually did the lion's share of the actual fighting." It was a calm, effective dismissal of a hoary national legend, and a few years earlier, Charles had dealt in the same unexcited but decisive fashion with the edifying fiction of the "unguarded frontier" and the pious misinterpretation of the Rush-Bagot Treaty. That treaty, he pointed out realistically in an article abstracted from his still unpublished *Armament and Disarmament in North America,* was followed "by an intensification rather than a slackening of general military measures." The building of border fortifications ended not in 1817 but in 1872: "before the latter year the unfortified frontier is pure myth."

The most brilliant and sustained example of this phase of Charles's work is *Quebec, 1759: The Siege and the Battle,* which appeared in 1959, the year of his retirement from the army and his return to academic life. Here was a subject admirably suited to his reasoning, critical, appraising manner. The siege of Quebec and the Battle of the Plains of Abraham were events of vast international importance, set against a backdrop of majestic natural beauty, enlivened by hazardous, theatrical episodes, and peopled by a group of highly individualistic and attractive personalities who frequently quarrelled with each other, and about whose characters and abilities historians and biographers had long disputed. Everything about this celebrated subject had encouraged the authors of an earlier day to revel in highly coloured prose, to heighten the dramatic intensity of the action, to take sides with one or other of the principal actors and to interpret the whole story with personal or national prejudice. It was some years now since anyone had seriously tackled the contentious theme; there was an accumulation of new evidence which nobody had investigated; and the bicentenary of the capture of Quebec was an appropriate moment for a serious reappraisal. Charles took excellent advantage of an inviting opportunity. And the epigraph on the title page of the finished book – "There would appear in this celebrated campaign fully as much guid luck as guid guiding" – was a clear indication of both his method and his conclusions. He was at his best – exact, temperate, judicious – in his examination and evaluation of the contending forces, the changing strategy and tactics, and the famous rival commanders, the overpraised and underrated Wolfe and Montcalm. "Both," he wrote in his final summing-up, "had some military talent. And the abilities of both have been grossly exaggerated by partial and sentimental historians writing under the spell of romantic circumstances in which two generals fought and died in that extraordinary campaign on the St. Lawrence two hundred years ago."

Quebec, 1759: The Siege and the Battle signalled Charles's return to historical subjects and daily occupations which were far removed from twentieth-century army history and army life. He enjoyed going back to undergraduate teaching, graduate supervision, committees, meetings, and discussions which, even after nineteen years' absence, still seemed so familiar. Yet he could not forget the army history, for it was still a major piece of unfinished work. He had agreed to take on the writing of Volume IV, the volume on inter-service war policies, as a part-time job; and in the light of previous experience, he suspected that it might be much more difficult to write honestly about policy than about operations. Twelve years before, in the crucial interview with Claxton, when the abandonment of the navy and air force histories seemed certain, the Minister of Defence had suggested that Volume IV in the army series should be converted into a volume on the war policies of the three armed services. Charles had insisted that such a comprehensive study could simply not be written without free access to the minutes of the cabinet and the War Committee; and on Claxton's recommendation, no less exalted a person than the Prime Minister, Mackenzie King, had approved the request for unrestricted consultation. Charles had made copious use of the cabinet records, but seven years later, when the publication of the first volume of the history was imminent, he was made suddenly aware of the fact that permission to consult was a very different thing from freedom to publish. He soon discovered that the civil servants in the East Block at Ottawa – members of the Privy Council Office as well as of the Department of External Affairs

- regarded their records with a special, almost mystical veneration. They acted, apparently, on the principle that the less of anything important there is to conceal, the more earnestly one conceals it. It was suggested by the irreverent that devout officials in External Affairs were accustomed to read despatches behind locked doors, with drawn blinds, by the feeble light of a low-powered electric torch. The civil servants in the Privy Council Office looked on cabinet records with the same awed mystique. To deal in familiar particularity with the proceedings of the cabinet and its committees seemed to them almost the equivalent of the profanation of sacred arcana. It would be far more appropriate, they thought, for an outsider like Charles to write simply and respectfully of the actions of the "Canadian government."

Charles had had a hard struggle to overcome this pompous, self-important aloofness. He had quickly realized that he would never succeed unless he propitiated the mandarins of the East Block by making some obeisance to the occult mysteries of the Privy Council Office; and he drew up a set of principles, based on practice in the United Kingdom, which he proposed to follow in his use of the cabinet records. Discussions in the cabinet or its committees, apart from actual decisions, were to be paraphrased, never quoted, and opinions expressed in cabinet meetings were never to be attributed to individual ministers. These provisions might seem to the uninitiated to be a more than adequate defence of the sacred fiction of cabinet unanimity and solidarity; but Louis St. Laurent, who some years before had succeeded King as Prime Minister, thought it necessary to add some still more circumspect precautions. The remarks made by guests of the Canadian government in cabinet discussions, he decided solemnly, must not be reported; and there must be no allusion to the "tone or atmosphere" of the meetings, since that might seem to suggest the dreadful possibility of Charles's profane presence in that holy of holies, the Council Chamber!

These restrictions had been a real embarrassment at the time of the publication of Volumes I and III of the history, but before Volume IV was ready to appear, they had lost a good deal of their restraining force. Charles went back to Ottawa, on leave of absence from the University of Toronto for the session 1965-66, to act as Director of History, Canadian Forces Headquarters. Apart from this one free year, however, the time he spent on the fourth volume had to be economized from a crowded academic schedule. The writing was, of necessity, a slow business; but, as Charles quickly realized, there were more advantages than disadvantages in a prolonged delay. After the lapse of a quarter-century, military and political security, which once seemed so essential, began to look unnecessary and even slightly ridiculous. Old soldiers and old politicians retire and write their memoirs, or die and leave their papers to the nation, and by degrees, the real materials for a history in depth are deposited in the public domain. The greatest gift of this slow but rewarding process was the diary of Mackenzie King, which was first published in an abbreviated form beginning in 1960, but which later became available to Charles in full. The diary was, of course, a private, not a public document. Its use was not governed by St. Laurent's absurdly stringent rules; and it was fuller, franker, and politically far more revealing – if less objective – than the cabinet records could ever be.

As the years went by and the documentary disclosures multiplied, the study projected for Volume IV began to acquire a greater depth and range of interest. Always implicit in the special examination of military policies is the study of national policy in general, both domestic and external; and now Charles could pursue these implications deeper into the men and issues of his period and backwards into their historical beginnings. He became familiarly acquainted with the personalities and views of the principal characters in his study and he had time to follow the twisted roots of Canadian foreign policy far back into the past. He found that Canada's ambiguous position in the British Commonwealth and the North American continent had their explanation in the steady advance of trends which could be discerned at least as far back as the first decades of the century. The paper he gave to the Royal Society in 1969, "From Meighen to King: The Reversal of Canadian External Policies, 1921-1923," and the essay he contributed to the Donald Creighton *festschrift*, "Laurier, King and External Affairs," are both evidence of this steadily widening interest in Canadian foreign policy.

Thus, when the fourth volume of the army history finally made its appearance in 1971, it was a different book from the inter-service policy volume which had been projected nearly fifteen years earlier. Even its name had been slightly altered; it was no longer designated as a numbered volume in a series. Its Virgilian main title, *Arms, Men, and Governments,* seemed to imply that it stood somewhat apart from its predecessors. Its main emphasis, of course, was still on military policy, and Charles's direct, straight-forward style had not been changed; but *Arms, Men, and Governments* had the dimensions and the political significance of a general history rather than of a specialized military study. Its account of the conscription crisis, which was the central domestic issue of the period, was more precise and detailed than any that had been published previously; but, naturally enough, it was in external relations, rather than in home affairs, that its greatest significance lay. It dealt realistically and unflinchingly with a war which, by the insistence of its demands and pressures, had exposed Canada's true character and her real position in the world at large. The fundamental tendencies which had guided her development in the past and were to dominate it in the future had now become clearly manifest. Henceforth Canada was to be that ambitious but ambiguous political entity, a "middle power" in a world governed by great powers and super-powers. The partnership which had been the aim of the old Imperial connection had been dropped forever, and a semi-colonial dependence had replaced it. The United States had triumphantly asserted its military and political hegemony over the whole North American continent, and Canada's attempt to defend its sovereign jurisdiction had been feeble and ineffectual. Charles had not sought to argue a thesis or to impose an interpretation on his readers: but his book brilliantly served the greater cause of historical truth and justice. His professed aim was to record events fully and honestly, in a comprehensive fashion, and with copious and exact detail. The incisive directness of his style, the critical realism of his approach and the sober humanity of his judgements, lifted his achievement far beyond these modest goals. *Arms, Men, and Governments* was a vast, but sharply detailed panorama which seemed to sum up Canada's past and to forecast its future.

Eugene Forsey:
Political Traditionalist,
Social Radical

My close association with Eugene Forsey, which has now lasted for
nearly thirty years, provides a convincing proof of the truth that
friendship does not necessarily depend upon propinquity. Eugene
was born in Grand Bank, Newfoundland, in 1904, and I nearly
two years earlier in Toronto. I grew up in my native city and
Eugene in Ottawa, to which he was brought, after the death of his
father, when he was only six months old. In the first decades of
this century, Canada's enormous distances were really divisive; the
capital of Canada seemed so far away and I never even set eyes on
it until I was in my late twenties. While Eugene crowned a brilliant
career at Ottawa Collegiate Institute, with thirteen firsts in Senior
Matriculation, I cut short my much less distinguished passage
through Humberside Collegiate, Toronto, at the Junior Matriculation level and left gratefully for Victoria College. Eugene read for
honours in Economics and Political Science and English at McGill
University, and I took the honour course in English and History
at the University of Toronto. We both graduated in 1925; but,
while Eugene remained another year at McGill and gained his
Master's degree, I departed at once for Balliol College, Oxford.
He followed me there a year later, having won the Rhodes Scholarship, which I failed to get in 1925, and it was at Balliol that we met
and talked for the first time. We saw relatively little of each other
then, however, for at Oxford, as at every other university, one's

Introduction to *Freedom and Order, Collected Essays of Eugene Forsey*, Carleton Library,
McClelland and Stewart, Toronto, 1974.

college year largely determined one's friends and acquaintances; and also, while Eugene chose the honour school in Philosophy, Politics and Economics, I read Modern History. Our time together at Balliol was brief, moreover, for while my Kylie Scholarship gave me only two years at Oxford, Eugene's Rhodes Scholarship provided for three. In 1927, I returned to Canada and began teaching in the Department of History at the University of Toronto, and two years later Eugene followed and became a lecturer in the Department of Economics and Political Science at McGill.

In the years that succeeded, we were separated almost as much by our contrasted interests as by the distance between Montreal and Toronto. The two major intellectual enthusiasms of Eugene's career – his constitutional traditionalism and his social radicalism – were by this time firmly established. His devotion to the constitutional inheritance bequeathed to Canada by British constitutional monarchy and the British imperial system had been nurtured by his paternal grandfather, W.C. Bowles, Chief Clerk of the Votes and Proceedings of the House of Commons, in whose home in Ottawa he had been brought up, and by Arthur Meighen, the political idol of his boyhood, whom he had often watched and heard with delight and admiration from the galleries of the House. During the years at McGill and Oxford, the political conservatism inherited from his family yielded to a growing interest in labour problems and a vigorous socialist faith. These new convictions were to prove very durable; but they did not disturb his belief in the British constitutional tradition and its great advocate, Arthur Meighen; and his first scholarly paper as a young McGill lecturer, which was presented to the Canadian Political Science Association in 1930, was called "The Royal Power of Dissolution of Parliament." This was a very early evidence of scholarly ability – my own first historical essay was not published until a year later – but productive scholarship and academic affairs could not alone have contented Eugene; and now, in the first harrowing years of the Depression, his socialist principles clamoured for active expression. The founding of the first democratic socialist party in Canada, the Co-operative Commonwealth Federation, had its chief intellectual inspiration in the work of the League for Social

Reconstruction, a body of scholars and teachers, most of them young, at McGill and the University of Toronto. Eugene Forsey, along with F.R. Scott and J. King Gordon, was one of the chief leaders of the Montreal group.

In all this activity I took almost no part at all. I remember attending what may very well have been the first meeting of the McGill and Toronto groups, which was held in the old Baldwin House, the history building at the University of Toronto. I think I sat through one session, or perhaps an entire day, of the discussions; but that was enough for me and I did not return and never became a member of the league. In those years, I was deeply involved in the study which was finally published as *The Commercial Empire of the St. Lawrence, 1760-1850,* and every moment not pledged to university teaching was devoted to that book. Its terminal date was 1850. I knew very little socialist theory, had little interest in contemporary Canadian politics, and was lamentably ignorant of modern Canadian history. It was not until *The Empire of the St. Lawrence* was published, and I went down to Ottawa in 1938 to join the research staff of the Royal Commission on Dominion-Provincial Relations, that I began to develop a real interest in Canadian Confederation and in post-Confederation history and public affairs. The long months I spent in Ottawa in 1938-39 brought my interests, sympathies, and beliefs much closer to those of Eugene. Indeed it could be said that the young men who worked for the Royal Commission and the young men who founded the League for Social Reconstruction shared a common concern for Canada in depression and a common hope for its better future. *Social Planning for Canada,* the book in which the league set out its proposals, offered a rigorously socialist programme. *The Report of the Royal Commission* was, of course, not nearly so radical in its recommendations; but it did lay down the bases of the interventionist and welfare state of the future. And both the book and the report assumed that the creation of the new Canada was a national enterprise which must be carried forward under the leadership of the federal government.

The gradual convergence of our interests and the curious near-coincidences of our careers continued. We both were awarded

Guggenheim Fellowships, Eugene in 1941 and I a year earlier. I was looking for a biggish subject, a sequel to my *Empire of the St. Lawrence;* and Eugene, having won his doctoral degree with a thesis on the royal power of dissolution of parliament, embarked on an even more ambitious project, a study of cabinet government in Canada. Research and writing had become a compulsive pursuit for both of us; but henceforth, we would follow it under markedly different circumstances. I returned, after my year as Guggenheim Fellow, to the traditional home of scholarship, the university; Eugene left it to take up a post as Director of Research in the Canadian Congress of Labour. For a few years, work on both our big projects was suspended. I turned aside to write a general history of Canada, and Eugene busied himself in cutting down his bulky thesis to the size demanded by his publishers, the Oxford University Press. In 1943, *The Royal Power of Dissolution of Parliament in the British Commonwealth* was finally published, with a foreword by Sir John Marriott. And it was this book, and the controversy which followed its publication, which first revealed Eugene's exceptional gifts to the general public of Canada.

The book itself, which surveyed the precedents of grant and refusal of dissolution throughout the British Commonwealth, reviewed the opinions of constitutional authorities on the subject, and then examined the Canadian constitutional crisis of 1926 in detail, was a classic example of the thoroughness, exactitude and trenchancy which characterized Eugene's historical method. It revealed his superb analytical and expository powers to the full; but other weapons in his intellectual armoury, his epigrammatic wit and controversial skill, did not appear in all their brilliance until the famous controversy with Dr. John Wesley Dafoe, the editor of the *Winnipeg Free Press.* It was inevitable that Dafoe should feel a compelling urge to attack Eugene's book. Along with O.D. Skelton and Professor R.M. Dawson, Dafoe had been one of the chief prophets and expositors of the Grit-Liberal interpretation of Canadian history, and he realized instinctively that this divine revelation was threatened by the impious heresy of Eugene's book. It was surely his duty, as well as his pleasure, to denounce it. Skelton was dead. Dawson who, after all, was a scholar as well as a

Liberal, might be swayed by the cogency of Eugene's case. But Dafoe, on the subject of the Grit interpretation of Canadian constitutional history, was proof against all argument and deaf to all reason.

He was a big, gross man, with a dogmatic, hectoring "bow-wow" manner, a truculent and abusive style, an intense partisan dislike to both Tories and socialists, and a psychotic hatred of what he thought of as "British imperialism." He cherished the journalist's favourite delusion that he was an authority on virtually everything; and for one class of subjects – Canadian political and constitutional history since Confederation – he regarded his pronouncements as ultimate and infallible. He had grown smugly accustomed to laying down the law for the respectful and edified citizens of western Canada; and, until he unwarily attacked Eugene's book, he may never have encountered an antagonist of anything like his own debating power. He soon discovered that he had aroused a formidable opponent, who was very unlikely to be intimidated by his air of bullying omniscience. On May 18, 1943, in a letter to the *Free Press,* Eugene charged that its review of his book was "compounded of about equal parts of misrepresentation and abuse" and proceeded to supply "five glaring examples" of these offences. The *Free Press* printed this letter, but Dafoe added a brief note accusing Eugene of having evaded his chief criticisms. He may have imagined that this was the end of the matter. He was mistaken.

On the identical and emphatic advice of the socialist T.C. Douglas and the Conservative Arthur Meighen, Eugene replied to Dafoe's taunt at length. Then began an exchange of letters which lasted through most of the summer and which, for sheer intellectual interest, was one of the best controversies in the history of Canadian journalism. From the beginning, Dafoe was completely outclassed. In neither historical knowledge, legal erudition, nor debating skill was he even remotely comparable to Eugene. He thrashed about, like a huge, infuriated bull, tormented by the banderillas of Eugene's incisive style and pointed wit. His laboured argument was a coarse mixture of historical inaccuracy, evasion, distortion, and abuse. Even the heavy bludgeon of his invective proved curiously ineffective against Eugene's easy command of all the literary weapons of controversy. Irony, satire, comic exaggeration, a copious knowledge of the rich vocabulary of denigration, were all brought into play as Eugene warmed to his work; and, in the end, Dafoe was revealed not only as an ill-informed and unreliable historian, but also as a prejudiced and narrow-minded political partisan. "I have never seen," Eugene summed up the indictment in one of his last letters, "a more glaring example of the lengths to which an inherently rotten case and blind partisanship can drive a man of ability, long experience in public affairs, and (hitherto) some reputation for intellectual honesty."

II

Although we saw each other occasionally at the annual meetings of the so-called "Learned Societies," it was not until the winter of 1944 that I received my first letter from Eugene. He wrote asking for some offprints of my essay "George Brown, Sir John Macdonald and the 'Workingman'," and he closed his letter by confessing to "a secret hope that you are writing either a life of Brown, or a life of Macdonald, or of both." This flattering encouragement could hardly have come at a more appropriate moment. By then I had abandoned my search for a sequel to *The Empire of the St. Lawrence,* and had decided to undertake a biography of Macdonald, which, though I scarcely realized it at the time, was perhaps the best answer to my quest. By the summer of 1944, I was deep in the researches which were to occupy nearly ten years of my life and which increasingly revealed how far Eugene and I shared similar attitudes to Canadian history. Even before I started work on the Macdonald biography, I had become suspicious of the Grit interpretation; but it was the neglect and underestimation of Macdonald by the Liberal historians of the early twentieth century that convinced me that their outlook was seriously distorting our understanding of the past. The result of this realization was an article "Macdonald and Canadian Historians," to which Eugene gave a hearty welcome. "The whole crew of Grits will froth at the mouth," he predicted, "and as they have had things so much their own way for so long, this rejoices me exceedingly.''

The close resemblance of our views on Canadian history and the Canadian constitution was converting a pleasant relationship into a friendship. We saw each other more frequently now, during Eugene's brief visits to Toronto and my longer periods of research in Ottawa. Our interests, of course, never coincided completely. During the last half of the 1940s, Eugene was very much occupied with the practical politics of the CCF. He ran as a CCF candidate in the Ontario election of 1945, and he opposed the redoubtable George Drew in Carleton County, in both the federal by-election of 1948, and the federal general election of the following year. I, on my part, was as little likely to give my ardent support to the CCF as I had been to become an active worker in the League for Social Reconstruction. I was anxious, of course, to see King's long reign brought to an ignominious close; but none of the opposition parties attracted me very much, for none of them seemed to share my deep concern at Canada's increasing subjection to the economic and political domination of the United States. My Canadian nationalism was perhaps more prickly than Eugene's, his social awareness more sensitive than mine.

Yet, although in many ways our interests differed, we agreed completely on the falsity and danger of Grit history and Grit constitutional theory; and thenceforth, from two quite different directions, we attacked it. Eugene laboured to strip King of the extravagant eulogy which had been lavished on him by Liberal apologists; I worked to rescue Macdonald from the disregard and obloquy to which Grit historians had subjected him. I was alone and unnoticed, for research and writing is a solitary business and I had no hope of exerting any influence on public opinion until my book was done. Eugene, who was an excellent platform speaker and an occasional contributor to popular weeklies such as *Saturday Night*, was a much more prominent and effective campaigner than I. Yet his task was inherently the more difficult of the two. The adulation of King, which had been rapidly swelling during the past years of the old leader's triumphant career, reached a climax in the lavish panegyrics which followed his death in 1950. For a

196

while, the stronghold of King's popular acclaim seemed impregnable. Yet Eugene worked steadily away towards its ultimate demolition. He ridiculed the dilatory and spasmodic fashion in which King had lived up to his grandiose pretensions as a social and industrial reformer. As a socialist, Eugene was deeply offended by these easy breaches of faith; but, on the whole, he was more seriously perturbed by King's repeated offences against the law and custom of the constitution.

He quickly became convinced that the real enormity of King's parliamentary career lay not so much in his individual constitutional misdeeds, as in his persistent attempts to undermine the moral and intellectual bases of the constitution in the minds of the Canadian people. Macdonald, he admitted, might have been guilty of corruption; "but," he continued, "I don't think he ever debauched the *mind* of the country as King has consistently done. In particular he never miseducated them about the constitution." What appalled Eugene was that at the bottom of all King's political machinations lay a complacent and cynical disregard of all law and custom, only excepting the unvarying law of his personal interest and partisan advantage. This general indictment was amplified, with many outrageous examples, in the paper delivered to the Canadian Political Science Association in the spring of 1951. King, Eugene concluded, believed not in parliamentary, but in plebiscitary democracy. He subscribed to the "demagogic heresy" that elections ultimately decide constitutional law and that a people can vote away its own liberties.

To deliver an academic address to an academic audience satisfied Eugene's scholarly standards; but it did not weaken the popularity of the King legend or challenge its journalistic supporters, or call in question the continuation of King's constitutional beliefs. King was dead; but his successors, the new generation of Liberal politicians, endorsed with equal fervour the Grit interpretation of history and the Grit theory of the constitution. Dafoe, King's principal constitutional apologist, was also dead, but he had left behind him a remarkable journalistic progeny: Dexter, Ferguson, and Hutchison, who ensured that orthodox Dafoeism, with its ring of booming authority, was certain to go on resounding through Canadian journalism. Two years after King's death, Bruce Hutchison published a biography of the former Prime Minister with the grandiose title *The Incredible Canadian,* and Eugene reviewed it in an Ottawa paper. The book opened with an oracular pronouncement to the effect that "the mystery of Mackenzie King" was not "the mystery of a man but the mystery of a people" and continued in this occult fashion for some time. Eugene, who enjoyed good rhetoric and was offended by spurious magniloquence, dismissed this incantation as "political crooning" and proceeded to supply an extensive list of the errors, omissions, and contradictions of Hutchison's book. This irreverent treatment aroused the ire of another journalist, Leslie Roberts, who assumed, like most newsmen, that mockery was the exclusive prerogative of the press and who wrote to *Saturday Night,* in a great flush of moral indignation, denouncing Eugene's "brutal" and "virulent" attack.

Eugene was admirably effective in these newspaper encounters. Yet to expose King and his apologists was not enough. King had set in motion certain definite tendencies in the political and constitutional development of Canada, and, under St. Laurent, these trends grew steadily in strength. The avowed aim of both men was Canadian national independence; and both men conceived it, not as the fulfilment of Canada's original and distinctive character, but as the repudiation of its past. For them Canada was not a constitutional monarchy which had attained complete sovereignty; but an unacknowledged republic which must now discard all tokens of its former "subjection" to its imperial master, Great Britain. The logical end of this process of rejection was the fall of the monarchy and the parliamentary system; but the Liberals sensibly realized that it was politically impossible to reach this ultimate goal. Canada's distinctive political character and constitutional identity could not be disavowed yet; but, in the meantime, it might be possible to prepare – very surreptitiously if need be – for the great day of their final repudiation by discarding the most conspicuous tokens and symbols of Canada's past and its historic connection with Great Britain.

Three of the symbols marked out for gradual elimination were the Union Jack in the fly of the Canadian ensign, the adjective "royal" in the names of a variety of Canadian institutions, organizations, and services, and Canada's original title the "Dominion of Canada." The word "Dominion," in particular, seemed to have aroused in King and St. Laurent a curious, almost pathological resentment; and ever since 1936 they had been systematically removing it from public documents and replacing it simply with the word "Canada," or the phrase "government of Canada." The title "Dominion of Canada" had, of course, been invented by Sir Leonard Tilley, and it was the deliberate and unanimous choice of the British North American delegates in London in the winter of 1866-67. The British government had nothing whatever to do with the title except to insert it in the British North America Act. Yet, despite these undoubted historical facts, Canadian politicians and leaders of public opinion helped to perpetuate the myth that the title was imposed on the reluctant British Americans by "Downing Street dictatorship." "Dominion," as Eugene pointed out, was "*our* word, perhaps the only distinctive word we have contributed to political terminology." It was inspired by a majestic verse in the seventy-second psalm; the sentiment of that verse was echoed in the sonorous Latin motto of the Canadian coat-of-arms, "*A mari usque ad mare,*" and no words could have described Canada's widespread boundaries with more beautiful precision. Yet, when public protest forced St. Laurent to make a statement in Parliament, he chose to belittle and disparage Dominion as a "colonial" locution which had grown shopworn and commonplace!

This unabashed defence of a deliberate attempt to obliterate the symbols of Canada's distinctive past alarmed Eugene. "The rot in our national life has gone so far," he wrote, "that government thought it could safely unveil its treason." The astonishing arguments, historically baseless and politically illiterate, by which Liberal supporters sought to defend the government's action, seemed equally shocking to him. He busied himself writing letters and short pieces to the newspapers, and participating in radio debates on the controversy; but he soon came to feel that these efforts were not enough. And he was fortunate in finding two people, Judith Robinson, a Toronto journalist, and John Farthing, a former master at Bishop's College School, Lennoxville, who shared his deep concern at the demoralization of Canadian public opinion. In the spring of 1952, they were planning to collaborate on a book on the British tradition in Canada, a book which, they hoped, would break "the Liberal grip on the intellectual life of the country." I, who was then giving all my time to the completion of my biography of Macdonald, readily agreed to contribute some passages from my essay "Sir John Macdonald and Canadian Historians."

The plan, as its authors had originally conceived it, was never carried out. The little book on the British tradition in Canada was too difficult a co-operative venture for three busy people. Yet their failure did not mean that constitutional monarchy and parliamentary government were left without historical explanation and theoretical defence; it did not mean that the "creeping republicanism" of the Liberals would proceed unquestioned and unchecked. In the middle 1950s, after four victories at the polls, it looked as if the professional Grit machine would continue indefinitely in Canada; but, in fact, after only two years more, it was brought to an abrupt stop. Two episodes in 1956 – the pipeline debate, which disclosed the depth of Canada's dependence on the United States, and the Suez crisis, which revealed the extent of her separation from Great Britain – together brought about its downfall. It was these two features of contemporary Canadian constitutional development – its easy susceptibility to American influence and its growing disregard for the British tradition – which had first aroused the fears of Eugene and his friends. They had detected these trends at an early stage and exposed the evasions which concealed their true significance; and, although the Forsey-Farthing-Robinson pamphlet was never completed, its authors' beliefs did not lack expression. Farthing died in 1954; but the theoretical work which was perhaps better suited to his talents, *Freedom Wears a Crown,* appeared three years later. Eugene continued to expound his own views in such articles as "The Crown and the Constitution"; and the two volumes of my biography of Sir John Macdonald came out in 1952 and 1955.

III

The new Conservative government had not been in power very long when another common, although different interest – the future of Canadian broadcasting – brought Eugene and me together again. Like Eugene, I was an infrequent radio listener and had not yet considered buying a television set; but, like Eugene also, I was deeply interested in the success of the national Canadian system. When Graham Spry, the Agent-General for Saskatchewan in the United Kingdom, returned to Canada to organize support for the reform and strengthening of national broadcasting, I was vulnerable to his persuasions. As far back as 1930, Graham Spry and Alan Plaunt had founded the Canadian Radio League and had successfully mobilized public opinion in favour of a nationally-owned broadcasting system. In 1957, twenty-one years after the founding of the Canadian Broadcasting Corporation, its thorough reconstruction seemed imminent; and from interviews with George C. Nowlan, the new Minister of National Revenue, Spry realized that the Conservative cabinet looked sympathetically on his plans. What was needed, he decided, and what would justify the government in its contemplated action, was a demonstration of popular support for the reorganization of Canadian broadcasting in the national interest. I was invited to join the movement on the assumption that my biography of Macdonald might give me a favourable hearing; and later, when Spry determined to revive the old Radio League under a new title, the Canadian Broadcasting League, I reluctantly agreed to act as its chairman.

On July 18, 1958, the executive of the league, supported by the representatives of a large number of national organizations, met with the Prime Minister and Messrs. Nowlan and Hees. Spry always insisted that this demonstration of public concern was of substantial use in strengthening the government's hand; and, in fact, the new Broadcasting Act, introduced a month later in the House of Commons, was a real departure from the past. It established – and this was an evidently essential reform – a national board which would regulate all Canadian broadcasting, public and private; and the board's declared object, as set out in the act, was a

201

"broadcasting service of high standard that is basically Canadian in content and character." The new system gave the Canadian Broadcasting League much, though by no means all, of what it had asked. Obviously a lot depended on the composition and conduct of the future board; and the league tried to exert some small influence on the appointment of its first members and to subject their original regulations to a critical review. The Canadian Labour Congress had given the league its powerful assistance, and we were all extremely pleased when Eugene was appointed one of the first members of the Board of Broadcast Governors. I continued for a while as Chairman of the league, trying rather unhappily to fill a position for which I was not qualified in any special way; and, in November 1959, when the board held a public hearing on its proposed new television regulations, I appeared before it as Chairman of the league's delegation. That was my last effort on behalf of Canadian broadcasting, for shortly after I accepted a post on the British Advisory Commission on the constitution of Rhodesia and Nyasaland, and left for Africa early in the new year. Eugene remained on the Board of Broadcast Governors for another two years. He thought well of his colleagues; he approved the board's policies in general; but he found the work, which had to be fitted in with the daily routine of his office in the Canadian Labour Congress, a heavy burden. In 1962, when he finally resigned over the issue of a television licence, he had reached the end of a distinct phase of his career. He left for a year at Queen's University, as Skelton Clark Fellow, to resume work on his history of Cabinet government in Canada. When he returned to the Canadian Labour Congress, it was to take up a new post as Director of a Special Project, the history of organized labour in Canada.

Tranquil years of research and writing seemed to stretch ahead for Eugene; but this pleasant prospect never quite became a reality. The 1960s were to confront him – and all students of Canadian government – with a constitutional challenge more serious perhaps than any that the twentieth century had yet produced. The long reign of Mackenzie King had brought many threats and injuries, acknowledged and concealed, to constitutional monarchy and parliamentary government; but the so-called "Quiet Revolution" in Quebec, which began with the triumph of the Liberals in the provincial election of 1960, carried with it an equally fundamental peril to Canadian national unity. The aim of the new French-Canadian nationalists was to preserve French Canada's identity and to strengthen and elevate its place in the Canadian nation. Obviously this object might be achieved in one of two quite different ways, either by promoting the equal partnership of the two founding races in the nation as a whole, or by recognizing the Province of Quebec as the real guardian of French-Canadian culture and by granting it legislative autonomy equivalent to a special or separate status in Confederation. Both these alternatives were so fraught with uncertainty, difficulty, and danger that a sober, clear-thinking people might have quailed before them; but a sober, clear-thinking people the Canadians emphatically were not, in the early 1960s. They existed in a state of confused exaltation, of muddle-headed euphoria. The French Canadians, who fondly believed that they had forced their hated English "oppressors" into submission, were flushed with the fervour of revolutionary achievement. The English Canadians, large numbers of whom had been lectured into believing that the pitiable state of French Canada was a crime of which they were morally guilty, were wallowing in the luxury of self-abasement, contrition, and repentance.

Eugene was not impressed by the excesses of this religious revival; but few of its self-righteous converts had a better knowledge and understanding of French Canada than he. His education in French had begun in elementary school; he could and did write and speak the language readily; he was an elder and steward in a French-Canadian United Church. He was ready to agree that there were two cultural traditions in Canada and that French-Canadian culture deserved more public recognition and support than it got; but he was convinced that this aim must be sought within a united and powerful Canada, and he refused to risk the country's dismemberment by the grant of separate or associate status to Quebec. That Canada was a nation of two cultures he had no doubt; but he was equally certain that this fact did not justify the use of the ambiguous phrase "two nations." Canada, he insisted, was politically and legally one nation and the adjective "national" was the proper word to describe its collective policies and enterprises. It was his emphasis on this vital distinction that led him to break with the New Democratic Party, the successor to the CCF, the party which he had served faithfully for almost thirty years. In the new party's constitution, which was presented to the founding convention in the summer of 1961, the word "national" had originally occurred no fewer than seventy-six times; but on the curious ground that it "hurt and offended our French-Canadian fellow citizens," this exactly appropriate adjective was deleted, and in many cases, though not all, the innocuous word "federal" was substituted instead. Disgusted with this ludicrous exercise in appeasement, Eugene quickly resigned from the new party. As he said later, the NDP founding convention was probably the only occasion in history when some thousands of people gathered to found a new national party and began by agreeing that there was no nation to found it in!

The grovelling submission of the NDP convention was a revealing example of the lengths to which the appeasers of French Canada were prepared to go and of the mindless excuses with which they justified their conduct. In loud, overbearing, and sanctimonious tones, they talked bad logic and worse history. The country resounded to a continuous babel which was popularly described as a "dialogue"; but it bore, in fact, not the slightest resemblance to a discussion in which two or more sides were engaged. On the contrary, it was a strident and raucous chorus in which French-Canadian nationalists and their English-Canadian sympathizers drowned all opposition and criticism. Those who objected that the rapid implementation of a programme of official bilingualism would be difficult and costly and might very well arouse resentment and dissension, were quickly and roundly denounced as bigots, racists, "WASPS" and "bad Canadians." Those who argued that such an official programme had no justification in Canadian history were categorically informed that, of course, it was amply justified by the "bicultural compact" of Confederation. The "bicultural compact" was, in fact, a complete myth; but the confident assertion of its authenticity, even by people who ought to have known better, was a curious index of the Canadians' ignorance of their own history. Repeatedly, Eugene and I had to trace our own way through the Charlottetown, Quebec and London conferences, through the British North America Act and subsequent Canadian history in order to prove that the "bicultural compact," even in modified form as a "moral commitment" or "extra-legal agreement," had no existence whatever.

Though he exposed the ignorance, and criticized the unrealistic excesses of the advocates of "instant bilingualism," Eugene continued to believe in a bilingual but united Canada. Within limits, he accepted the first method of preserving French Canada's identity and strengthening its position in Canada. He almost totally rejected the second method, the recognition of the Province of Quebec as the only effective guardian of French-Canadian culture and its elevation to a separate or independent status. He readily conceded that Quebec was a different province, distinguishable in several important ways from the others. He had no objection to its takeover of all social security programmes which lay within provincial jurisdiction. But, in fact, the claims of the province, or of its principal theorists, went much further than this. Some demanded the transfer of considerable amounts of unquestionably federal jurisdiction, as well as fundamental changes in the composition, organization, and functions of two basic federal institutions, the Senate and the Supreme Court. Others urged a Canadian Confederation composed of two sovereign associated states, Quebec and the rest of Canada. In Eugene's opinion, all these plans would prolong Canada in a mangled existence that would be worse than death. He preferred Quebec's complete separation preceded by "hard bargaining."

Eugene and I began to feel somewhat isolated amid the rapidly growing clamour for the appeasement of French Canada; and this feeling increased after 1965, when we both joined the Ontario Advisory Committee on Confederation, a small committee established by the provincial government to offer advice on the issues of Canadian federalism, advice which could, of course, be either accepted or rejected. It soon became clear that we would frequently be in a minority in the committee, sometimes, indeed, a minority of two. Our own views had been formed by this time; and the equally firm opinions of some other members might have been inferred from their previous or subsequent activities. Professor John Meisel of Queen's University had been one of the supervisors of research for the Royal Commission on Bilingualism and Biculturalism. Professor Paul Fox of the University of Toronto later took part in the delimitation of the bilingual districts set up by the Official Languages Act; and President T.H.B. Symons of Trent University subsequently acted as commissioner for an inquiry into French-language secondary education in Ontario. The position of the senior member of the Committee, Professor Emeritus Alexander Brady, could not perhaps be so readily deduced from the record. In 1940, when the findings of that other great inquiry into Canadian federalism, *The Report of the Royal Commission on Dominion-Provincial Relations,* was published, Professor Brady seemed to be a convinced centralist. In a long review of the Commission's Report, he doubted the wisdom of its recommendation that residual authority in the social services should remain with the provinces. "The true end of Canadian development," he wrote, "must be national unity with such centralization of legislative power and decentralization of administrative discretion as the necessities of statehood at the time dictate." That was in 1940. Twenty-five years later, it appeared that "national unity" and "centralization of legislative power" were not, after all, "the true end of Canadian development." Times had changed and Dr. Brady had changed with them. For several reasons, including the "dynamism of a fresh and potent French-Canadian nationalism," the federal pendulum had swung, and Professor Brady was determined to swing with it!

In the years 1965-1970, the conciliation of Quebec through constitutional change and administrative adjustment was a cause which rolled steadily forward by its own momentum. The strength of its current was very evident inside the government and civil service of Ontario. What the people of Ontario thought about the subject was a question which didn't seem to awaken much interest in governmental circles. Among the many documents with which the members of the Advisory Committee were supplied was a monthly compilation of reports and editorials on Confederation, taken from the French-Canadian press. Apparently it never occurred to the secretariat that a monthly collection of English-Canadian or Ontario views on Confederation would serve any useful purpose. And when, in the autumn of 1967, Prime Minister John Robarts announced that a "Confederation of Tomorrow" .conference would be held in Toronto, it would have been difficult to prove that he had acted in response to an urgent appeal from the people of his province. He had, however, created a fashion which the federal government felt obliged to follow. A few months later, it summoned an official constitutional conference; and the Province of Ontario, with the aid of its Advisory Committee, began to prepare its views for submission. In these later sessions of the Committee, Eugene was at his best, speaking to the point in his concise and vigorous fashion, and writing a stream of comments, memoranda, and papers.

In 1970, when Mr. William Davis succeeded Mr. John Robarts as Prime Minister of Ontario, the work of the Advisory Committee came to a close. Eugene might have fancied himself freed at last from the organized investigation of constitutional change; but if so, he was quickly undeceived. In the autumn of that year, he was summoned to the Senate of Canada; and he soon found himself appointed as a senatorial member on the Special Joint Committee of the Senate and the House of Commons on the Constitution of Canada. He became an active and influential member of this committee; but he soon discovered that at Ottawa – as at Toronto – constitutional amendment was conceived almost exclusively in terms of purely contemporary values, interests, and concerns. When, on occasion, witnesses before the committee tried to talk historically, their object seemed to be to misrepresent the origins of Confederation and to disparage its authors, and they dealt largely in synthetic mythology and vulgar folklore. To Eugene's great disappointment, nobody who could give adequate expression to the historical point-of-view, had appeared before the committee; and, at his earnest request I went down to Ottawa in the spring of 1971 to give evidence. I came away convinced that I had wasted my own time, as well as that of the committee. Its members were about as interested in the plans of the Fathers of Confederation as they would have been in the laws of Hammurabi or the constitutions of Solon. What really seemed important to them were what they called "the constitutional imperatives" of the moment – meaning, I suppose, the political pressures of the 1960s.

In due course, the committee's report was completed and printed, and Eugene discussed it ably in a critical speech in the Senate. More than a year has gone by since then, and the great new constitution which the committee had devised has yet to become the law of the land. Canadians were urged by its authors, "to press with us for the writing of a new Constitution"; but, in fact, all real hope of a new constitution had vanished, when what might have been called its first instalment, the Victoria Charter, was deliberately rejected by Quebec, the province which it had been specially designed to satisfy. The movement for constitutional change, which had been both originated and terminated by Quebec, and which had lasted for ten years of barren agitation, ended at last in frustration and futility.

IV

Eugene Forsey has occasionally been heard to say that he lacks the "staying power" needed to complete a large historical or political work. This is, of course, demonstrably untrue. He has published one very influential constitutional study, *The Royal Power of Dissolution of Parliament*. His history of trade unions in Canada is now finished; and, with the greater leisure which he now enjoys, he may soon complete his book on Cabinet government. Time is the indispensable requisite of research and writing; and, for long periods of his life, Eugene has not had a great deal of it to use as he likes. Scholarship is also a solitary business, carried on in archives and libraries, where the rumour of contemporary affairs is dim; and Eugene has always been irresistibly interested in contemporary affairs. His socialist faith, as well as his position as Director of Research for the Congress of Labour, has focused his attention on social questions and labour disputes. His historical knowledge and his firm belief in the significance of history for modern politics has led him into innumerable debates and controversies. He has responded rapidly and with great address to these constantly recurring challenges, and the result has been a long succession of letters to newspapers, short pieces in periodicals, essays in learned journals, and papers delivered to university audiences. This became, in the end, the mode of expression which he liked best and by which he is best known.

What strikes his reader at once is the extent and particularity of Eugene's knowledge, and the systematic and logical way in which it is organized. His erudition is at once enormous in its range and minute in its detail. If he has ever been caught out in an important mistake of fact, I don't know when or where it occurred; and I am completely confident that he has never written a muddled or slip-shod piece of prose in his life. His thoughts are always marshalled in their most effective order, and the argument proceeds rigorously from stage to stage towards an inescapable conclusion. A sharp and censorious eye is alert to mistakes – his own or other people's – in the evidence or the style; and a number of Canadian historians and political scientists have benefited – and also suffered on occasion – from the lists of errata that Eugene has discovered in their work. I used sometimes to be sent copies of these formidable lists, and I was so impressed with his critical exactitude that I asked him to perform the same service for me – before, not after, publication! He read the manuscript of *Canada's First Century* with his usual scrupulous care, and I still possess the copious pages of his corrections and comments. Nobody can rival him in this field, for nobody possesses such an exact and comprehensive knowledge and such an acute and sensitive feeling for words.

Erudition and precision are the first requirements of constitutional history; but there are other, equally desirable qualities that Eugene displays in his historical writing. His prose is not only exact and lucid, it is also continuously lively. He could hardly write a dull page if he tried! His sentences are crisp, incisive, forceful, obviously the work of a man to whom words come easily, who has a vast knowledge of English history and literature, and who savours their most memorable episodes, passages, and phrases. Quotations, acknowledged and unacknowledged, from the Bible,

Shakespeare, and Milton, down to P.G. Wodehouse, make their unobtrusive but effective appearance in his pages. Political anecdotes, from the days of Pitt and Palmerston down to those of Churchill, Borden and Mackenzie King, lend a piquant savour to his writing. The entire gamut of the critic and controversialist – wit, satire, irony, comic exaggeration, burlesque and invective – are all available at his command. He can rise to great heights of angry rhetoric as in his denunciation of J.W. Dafoe; he can compose a set of comic rhymed couplets at the expense of some silly journalist or the half-baked advocates of a Canadian republic or a "distinctive" Canadian flag. His metaphors and turns of phrase are deft and amusing. "Even in his loftiest flights of oratory," he wrote once of Mackenzie King, "he always carries a verbal parachute, so that he can bail out if things get too hot for him." King has been a constant inspiration to Eugene's powers of parody, both spoken and written. He can mimic King's earnest, nasal tones, and his long, dribbling casuistic sentences so well that on one occasion at least, his voice was mistaken for King's own on the radio!

As a historian and political scientist, Eugene stands quite alone in Canada. His combination of scholarly and literary qualities is unique. His historical traditionalism and social radicalism form an incomprehensible mixture which completely baffles most Canadian critics. They are simply not equipped, intellectually, to cope with him. Literary criticism in Canadian newspapers normally reads as if it had been written by journalists who had been given the job of literary editor as a reward for the competent reporting of the police court or the town council. Political and social criticism, even in Canadian periodicals and learned journals, is all too frequently the work of commentators and scholars, whose narrow specialized knowledge is not enlarged by general cultivation and lacks any real sense of discrimination. In far too many cases, these critics summarily divide historians and political scientists into categories according to the names of existing political parties, or the popular designations of current political and social attitudes. On a higher level, they are labelled as liberals, conservatives, or socialists, and placed firmly in the appropriate pigeonholes. On a lower level, they are tagged as Reds, Tories, "WASPS," bigots, and "imperialists," and usually derided. Occasionally, even to the undiscerning Canadian critic, all existing labels seem unsuitable for one reason or another. This makes the critic acutely unhappy, and his usual way out of the difficulty is to invent a new label by the simple method of hyphenating two of the old ones! "Red-Tory," a typical example of this clumsy attempt at refined analysis, is a term which might conceivably, I suppose, be bestowed on Eugene. A more inadequate, inappropriate, and misleading term could scarcely be imagined! The truth is that he is indecipherable by Canadian criticism. If only there were more Canadians like him!

Other Books
by Donald Creighton

The Empire of the St. Lawrence 1937
Dominion of the North 1944
John A. Macdonald, Volume I: *The Young Politician* 1952
John A. Macdonald, Volume II: *The Old Chieftain* 1955
Harold Adams Innis: Portrait of a Scholar 1957
The Story of Canada 1959
The Road to Confederation 1962
Canada's First Century 1970
Towards the Discovery of Canada 1972
Canada: The Heroic Beginnings 1974
The Forked Road: Canada 1939-1957 1976
Takeover 1978